The
PRICE
of Faith

Our Journey Together
with the Holy Spirit

The Price of Faith
Our Journey Together with the Holy Spirit
By Colleen Price

Printed in the United States of America

Published by: Michael Young Publishing

FORWARD

Perhaps, once in a life-time, you may have the opportunity to meet some really special people. People who, because of the call of God on their lives, will impact your life forever.

Stuart and Colleen Price are such people!

When I first heard the story of how God had spoken to them about Arkansas, all the way on the other side of the world in Australia, I was overwhelmed!

For those of us who live in Arkansas, we know what a treasure it is. In fact, it's one of America's best kept secrets! From our beautiful mountains, lush rivers valleys, and fertile farm lands, most of us who live here have a passionate love for our state. And for decades we have been hearing countless prophecies of how God is going to send an Outpouring of His Holy Spirit to Arkansas that will touch the world.

So just imagine how we felt when we learned that God had spoken about us to someone so far away and then sent them here as His Ambassadors to show us His Great Love! I never tire of hearing the story of how it all came about! It's a story of perseverance in the face of many obstacles. It's an account of the many sacrifices they made to answer the call of God on their lives. It's a picture of great faith as they ventured into the unknown. And it is an example to us all, of the amazing things God can and will do if only we are willing and obedient.

It has been a joy and an honor to help get this amazing and unique story into the hands of as many people as possible. Adventure awaits as you dive into this wonderful account of two lives who learned…. "The Price of Faith"

Debbie Young
Author/Evangelist

In the months leading up to the year 2000, many intercessors and I, in the state of Arkansas, were seeking God for revival in our communities and throughout the state.

Whenever I heard that the Spirit was moving in a church I would make every effort to attend, seek more of God, and be a part of what He was doing.

In March of 2000 I learned from an intercessor there was to be a meeting in North Little Rock and that a couple, Stuart and Colleen Price from Australia, would be ministering. This couple had left their country in obedience to God's call to come to Arkansas. I had to go to North Little Rock!

Late in the afternoon a friend knocked on my door. He said he had been trying to contact me all day and he placed some money in my hand, money that would buy gas for my car.

Even though I knew I would be late to the meeting I headed there. When I arrived, I found one empty seat in the center of the front row. After brother Price finished his message he called for those who wanted prayer. I jumped up and was the first one to be prayed for. Down I went under the Power of God!

What a privilege and a blessing it has been to get to know Stuart and Colleen Price and to have played a small part in what God was doing in Arkansas through their ministry. Their lives and their ministry have influenced my life as well as the life of my wife, Julia.

I have witnessed miracle after miracle as they have allowed God to work through them. They are just ordinary people who have faith in an Almighty God and were obedient when they heard the word, "Arkansaw" You will be blessed and challenged as you read about the wondrous things God has done!

Duane R. Amis
Pastor

ACKNOWLEDGEMENTS

First of all I want to acknowledge our dear friend and author, Debbie Young. It has been her encouragement and enabling that has brought this to fruition.

Debbie knew nothing of previous prophetic words spoken over me for many years. The task seemed impossible for me, but God made it all possible with Debbie's help.

Also, to Michael Young Publishing, what a God-send you are! I am so grateful for all your help. Thank you for using your skills to bring this to pass.

Thank you, Ken Wigglesworth, pastor and author, who prophesied this book into being. Sometime later, when he was encouraging me to begin writing, he gave me the title calling it, "The Price of Faith".

DEDICATION

Without Jesus Christ in our lives and His enablement, faithfulness, and calling there would be no story. I want to acknowledge the Holy Spirit (the Helper) who has empowered us to fulfill the call since our salvation in 1973.

I dedicate this book to my collaborator and darling husband of fifty-eight years. Stuart and I have made a great team and have enjoyed our lives together with its many challenges and adventures. We've laughed, we've cried, we've stood on His Word and It's promises together, and have seen God move mountains before us!

I also dedicate this book to our three children: Alan, Raymon, and Sarah, our fourteen grandchildren, and five great-grandchildren. It is our legacy to them all.

Blessings,
Colleen and Stuart

PREFACE

To bring glory to God in our life's journey and to show His faithfulness to us over the past 50 years.

To leave a legacy for our family and the generations to come.

TABLE OF CONTENTS

INTRODUCTION

Prayer and fasting have played a key part in seeking the Lord for His direction in our lives. This has always been the case for over 50 years.

We have always been obedient to His plan and calling. Jesus says,

> *"Without Me, you can do nothing." John 15:5b*

> *"In all your ways acknowledge Him. And He shall direct your paths." Proverbs 3:6*

> *"A man's heart plans his way, but the Lord directs his steps." Proverbs 16:9*

However, after the Lord spoke, "Arkansas", our prayers elevated to a whole new level! People in our church began to pray with such fervency, like never before. We were not a large church but many times we would have 75 people who gathered to pray. People would come from other churches to join us in prayer. God was moving powerfully in our midst.

Unbeknown to us, the intercessors in the state of Arkansas were also praying, and had just established a whole network of intercessors throughout the State over the internet. The late Reverend Ruth Finley played a major part in this.

God was beginning to open a door!

Chapter 1
New Beginning

"This is your Year of Jubilee", the Holy Spirit whispered in my ear. "What does that mean?" I thought. Year of Jubilee, 50 years. I understood that. The penny dropped.

It was March 7th, 1973 when I first gave my heart to the Lord. How fantastic that was! I was so excited to realize this, and the anniversary was the following week. I could have easily missed celebrating the anniversary with the busyness of life.

What a lot has happened from that starting point in Wanganui, New Zealand where I attended an Assembly of God Church with my 62 year old widowed mother, Norah Houten, and gave my heart to the Lord.

My darling Dad had died and was buried on my 23rd Birthday. I was now 26 years old. It was a pivotal decision in my life, that totally changed everything. I embraced it with joy. I had a wonderful husband, Stuart, and two little boys: Alan who was 4 years old and Raymon who was 2 years old. I had just lost a baby in December after carrying it for 5 1/2 months. My life had been hard after that loss and I had battled depression as a result.

As a young person, I had been involved in The Methodist church in Woodville, my hometown, and I loved going to Sunday School and church. I could say I had always had a great love for the Lord and the church.

The Methodist parsonage was next door to my parent's home and also my grandparents, so I had always played with the minister's children. I had been very much at ease with their parents.

In my school years I attended, Every Girls Rally, which was run by the Brethren and I learned lots of Bible verses for my memory badges. There was nothing I liked better.

Mum and Dad moved to Wanganui when dad retired. I was plunged into a new city and began working in 1964. I met Stuart not long after, and strangely enough we worked alongside one another. Stuart worked for Wanganui Motors (Ford dealership) as a mechanic and I worked for a Stock and Station Company called Freeman R. Jackson. After some time, I became the head Bookkeeping Machinist (before computers were on the scene).

I was sixteen and he was seventeen when we met. We never dated anyone else. We married when I was nineteen, and Stuart, twenty. We built our new home after eighteen months and celebrated Stuart's twenty first birthday there. In order to obtain a mortgage one had to buy land, and we did this. Stuart was finishing his apprenticeship on a small wage, but I had been able to save well in a good paying job. We were under-age to apply for the mortgage, so the application had to be approved by a Judge. We were very nervous, and after a line of questioning he approved our loan for the maximum of $6,000. Now we were free to search for plans and ready to build. What an achievement it was! The Judge congratulated us and wished us well.

After my acceptance of Christ in 1973, things changed in our household. Stuart plunged from a very happy man to one that struggled with allowing me to attend one church service on a Sunday, and no mid-week Bible Studies.

Life was difficult to say the least, but I loved my husband dearly and prayed every day for his salvation. While Stuart slept, I laid hands on him and believed.

He attended church a couple of times and came to a water baptism. A lady insisted on us sitting near the front, and Stuart resisted her requests. He told me that if he didn't sit at the back of the church he was leaving and would never come back. I was forbidden to ever invite him again. Of course, my desire was to get water baptized, but it didn't sound like he would attend with me.

The Lord was doing some marvelous things in my life and my mother and I shared everything. We loved being together but we had to be wise in what we talked about in front of Stuart. One lunch time after we returned from church, Stuart slapped his hand down on the table and shouted, "God will not be talked about at this meal time!" We were quiet around the table and felt miserable. However, as soon as the meal was over and Stuart left to work outside, we were free to talk.

In retrospect, I can tell what I discovered many years later. Stuart was preaching in the Assembly (Faith Community Church as it was known then) and he had become a real evangelist and loved sharing his testimony. Little did I know what had transpired after that lunch that fateful day. He went on to tell how he had sat under the kitchen window and listened intently to our conversation about the Lord, and all that He was doing in our lives.

How I wished that I would have had some encouragement in those difficult days! I kept a lot locked up on the inside. Even though I was close friends with the pastor's wife, I wanted everyone to like Stuart when they got to know him. I had faith that he would accept Jesus and that we would be equally yoked.

One day, while on the altar believing for my man to be saved, I saw a silhouette of a man with hands raised, praising God. It totally changed the way I prayed for Stuart. I thanked God for his salvation and I said, "Stuart is on his way!" Every time things became difficult at home I secretly thanked the Lord, "He's on his way." I later realized that this was a great key — praising God for something in advance and believing that this would indeed happen.

Things became worse in our marriage, but I continued to thank the Lord for Stuart's salvation. I had to take my hands off and give full control to the Lord. I had to believe, and trust, and love my man. One may never understand the battle that is raging on the inside, and male pride will never make it known. The Lord was working in Stuart's life, and the Lord was answering my prayers. All I had to do was believe.

Many times I would come home after a wonderful night at church and face an angry man. His words would wound and cut me, and I would go to bed crying. He had allowed me to go to the service but was not happy about it.

I didn't always understand about the clash of the kingdoms. Stuart was fighting Jesus. I didn't understand that there was a call on Stuart's life, and that he would later preach and be used in the Kingdom. It seemed the more I prayed, the worse he became.

Stuart's salvation was foremost on my mind. I thanked God daily for my precious man. God had shown me the silhouette and I had to believe God was at work. I was forbidden to ever invite him to church again. How God would do it, I didn't know, but I believed He would do it.

Chapter 2
By Faith

We had a visiting evangelist from Australia, and he was preaching a lot of services in the church. Mother and I had gone, and on the Thursday night there was no meeting.

I knew Stuart was entertaining the men from the Ford Motor Company on that night and I was hoping I would be able to attend a couple of meetings before the Crusade finished on the Sunday.

I settled the children down for the night and prepared to have a quiet night at home with my knitting. At 9:00pm, I heard someone coming in the front door. It was Stuart and he was as white as a sheet, and not happy.

I said, "What is wrong, have you had an accident?" He pushed past me and headed for the bedroom, obviously upset and started getting ready for bed. "No", he said abruptly. "Tomorrow night we're going out."

"Stuart, you knew I wanted to go to church tomorrow night", I said. I was sure he had planned to go to a party, or something like that. "Shut up", he said, "That's where we are going!" Well now I had lots of questions to ask. He had forbidden me to ever ask him to church again, and I had respected that. Now he says we're going to church! It was not a good time to ask too many questions, so I had to accept that, as Stuart was determined to get to sleep.

I discovered (not in very much detail at that point) that he had met the pastors and the evangelists and all their wives while they were dining out at the best restaurant in town. That was exactly where Stuart had taken the Ford Company representatives with the firm's cheque book and were having a night on the town. He spotted them as he entered the dining room and walked past their table, ignoring them, feeling very uncomfortable.

He ordered the meals with his guests and excused himself to go outside into the fresh air. "Pull yourself together Stuart", he was saying, breathing deeply. Stuart was feeling sick. It was unlike him to ignore people he knew. But he saw Pastors from his few visits to church, and here they were, spoiling his night out.

After he'd pulled himself together, he returned to the direction of his table but could not ignore the group of Pastors again. He walked right over to speak to them, acting like he had just seen them. They sprang up from their seats very happy to chat and introduced him to Pastor Clark Taylor, the evangelist from Australia, who wouldn't stop shaking his hand.

The evangelist had no idea that Stuart was unsaved, and proceeded to tell him about all the great things the Lord was doing. Next thing, Stuart heard himself say, "Tomorrow night, I'll come to hear you!" At this, Stuart felt ill. The conviction of the Holy Spirit was heavily upon him. "What do I do now?", he thought. "I have forbidden Colleen to ever invite me, and now I've committed myself to going to church."

7

He returned to his guests, and the dinner was served. This was at his most favourite restaurant with his favorite meal, a beautiful steak! Stuart arose from the table and was feeling in a very panicked state. All he could do was drive home and go to bed to get away from this terrible churning of conviction on the inside.

"I must get to sleep", he thought. He'd left his guests to spend the rest of the evening on their own, and what's more, they had to pay the bill, or as Americans say, the check. He knew he would have to face his boss at the dealership the very next day! How could he explain this?

I now understand the whole story of the happenings from this fateful night and Stuart was hoping he would be called up-country and would not be able to attend church, as promised. He told me he hoped he would be feeling sick, which would excuse him of the commitment. However, none of these things happened. The Lord sure had him on a hook!

Friday night, Stuart worked till 7:00 pm and it was planned that I would collect him from work. He cautioned me that if I told anyone where we were going, he would not come. Stuart had always been a person of his word. In his selling of tractors and farm machinery and later cars etc., if he promised something, he would always do it! That's why this commitment to come, was unbreakable. He was a man of his word.

We drove to the auditorium and not much was spoken. The atmosphere was tense. As we walked up the hill to the entry of the Davis Lecture Theatre, I said to him, "The least you can do is smile. These people are my friends."

He snapped back, "I'm not smiling, and they are not my friends." Oh dear! This was going to be a difficult night, and I was so looking forward to being in service again. He retorted, "A man needs his head read, coming to this place."

A dear elderly man greeted us with a smile and a handshake, and Stuart wouldn't even take his hand. Stuart just gave a grunt. He insisted that we head up to the rear of the auditorium, otherwise he was leaving. I had no option so I just followed. His body language said it all. One could see he didn't want to be there. I'm sure it was obvious to others as well.

The worship was wonderful, and the service was dynamic but I was so aware of the body language beside me, and thought, "Maybe next time Lord."

Pastor Clark Taylor gave an altar call and many responded. He said, "There is someone up the back having a spiritual battle. The Lord is calling you, and the devil is saying, 'Stay where you are'. Pray for this person." So we all prayed. I was unaware that this was happening right beside me! This was the answer to my prayers.

I still had my eyes shut when my friend tapped my arm and said, "Look, there's Stuart!" He had gone to the altar. I felt numb. It was hard to believe! Stuart had a long way to walk and he had done it alone! I was struggling. I thought, "When my husband gets saved, I am going to be so happy." This was something else.

Stuart was taken out by one of the counselors, and then came back into the meeting. He looked so happy! I have never seen such a sudden change in a man. He was transformed into a new man before my eyes. I think I was in shock, after the battle that had taken place over the past seven months. It was not very long, but very intense.

The next day, he couldn't wait to return to church. It was astounding! That night they called for people who wanted the baptism of the Holy Spirit. He didn't have a clue what that was but had this simple thought, "If God is giving it, I want it!" He stood at the altar and saw others being slain in the Spirit. "I'm not doing that", he thought. Pastor Clark prayed for him, and down he went! A pastor called up to me saying, "He's speaking in tongues!" I still felt in shock!

This man had stopped me from attending meetings for all those months, and now he was hungry for God and wanted to attend everything! An adjustment was certainly needed in my life, and I realized what God had done. Now, we were equally yoked. Thank you, Jesus! We certainly loved one another. Tears flowed when we discussed all that had happened.

The following Monday at work, Stuart was called to the boss's office. He was raked over the coals for leaving the guests at the restaurant and disappearing, leaving them to pay the bill. There was very little he could say. He wasn't about to say that God had been on his case. So he just said, "It's personal and I cannot tell you anymore." Thankfully, the boss accepted that as Stuart was one of his reliable workers.

We loved the Lord together and became fully involved in the church, learning and growing in leaps and bounds. Stuart studied the Word every day, and the Holy Spirit was the driving force in his life. We prayed and studied together, knowing that this was the strength in our lives.

People gravitated to Stuart for prayer right from the start, and he helped so many: counseling, teaching, and assisting the pastor in the church. Nothing was too much for him. He became Youth Leader; then we grew a Home Group in our home that met for many years.

Even today, we still have contact with many people of whom we were instrumental in their spiritual growth in the church in Wanganui. We had such a genuine love for the congregation, and indeed it was becoming so much a part of our lives. The church was a beautiful family in the community. Even so, there was little encouragement from the pastoral team and some things were very disparaging. Stuart always said, "My life is in the Lord's Hands and He will have the final say."

I could see what was happening and felt hurt by pastor's comments that always said that Stuart had little education and would never pastor. They always said Colleen would be a great pastor's wife, but that was so hurtful, especially to me. We were a team, and always worked as one. Stuart encouraged me often, saying, "Don't let these things get in your spirit. They will make you bitter. Handle them at arm's length." I felt like screaming. I heard these words so often. Stuart said, "Please don't take my hurt, I can handle it."

Every two years, the Lord would give us something to hold onto. It brought strength and encouragement to us both. It was strange that New Zealand was known for its prophets, and prophecy was so strong from visiting speakers. They prophesied freely over the congregation, but never over us. God was teaching us to stand on His Word and believe His promises. Sometimes we don't see God's hands in these things at the time, but in retrospect it becomes clear. It was never a thought in our minds to change churches. We were fully committed at Faith Community, loved our church and all who were in it.

Life certainly had many challenges and dealing with our emotions was a part of it. Stuart had this sense that the Lord was taking us to Australia, almost right from the time of his salvation. Other members of his family had moved to Western Australia. His twin Cecily, and his sister Jacqui were living there.

Stuart was such a witness in his workplace, Wanganui Motors. He advanced from mechanic to A-Grade Mechanic, to Farm Tractor Service, then Sales, and then into the showroom and in a suit.

He loved visiting the farmers in their own environment on the farms, as he was brought up on a farm with his family. He was very shy. Prayer, and the Holy Spirit were a big force to help Stuart overcome.

Every week on the outskirts of Wanganui, Stuart would visit the Fordell sale yards. There were farmers everywhere, and of course this provided a wonderful opportunity for potential sales of tractors, machinery and new vehicles.

Each week Stuart would try to talk to himself, and draw strength to face these men, many well known to him. Sometimes he was unable to get out of the car, and I later learned that he drove back into the city more than once, weeping at his inability to overcome. All of this was previous to his salvation.

We know that God hasn't given us a spirit of fear, but of love, and power and a sound mind. In order to overcome his fear, next time he drove out to the sale yards, he spoke in his heavenly language and prayed all the way. On arrival, he boldly stepped out of the car and approached the farmers, many happy to greet him as they knew him well. That day of overcoming was a memorable one he will never forget. He bought a bull, along with another farmer, which would fill our freezer and also sold a new tractor We were so excited, especially Stuart.

Chapter 3
Pressing Through Fear

I had re-entered the work force again after raising our children in our home. I was a homemaker at heart, and when many ladies were sick I would prepare a dinner for the family. I got so much joy out of being able to do this. However, I had such a love for real estate. Stuart encouraged me to talk with a lady realtor to ask her about it.

There was major unspoken problem that I would have to grapple with. I had struggled with a stammer all my life, and fear kept me bound up. From the age of three this had developed. I struggled to read aloud in school and all throughout my years at Tararua College I was very quiet and lacking in confidence.

These years at college were very happy. I participated in School Choir, and two Gilbert & Sullivan School Productions. What a joy it was! I found singing was easy and no stammer was evident, which built my confidence immensely. However, in speech, my stammer was more prominent. Nervousness dominated my life and indeed hampered it. The telephone was also another problem. I tried not to use it. How was I ever going to cope with real estate?

The day I went to speak with the realtor, I was very nervous. I was embarrassed that she had her other sales ladies gathered in her office as well. When I walked out of the office, I had, in my hand, a real estate diary and a job!

I was very excited initially, then fear set in! All those old fears overtook me and I was going to have to overcome all of them, with the Lord's help. I was so scared. There were a bunch of them. Revelation 12:11 says, "They overcame him by the blood of the lamb…" I was going to have to overcome all my fears.

Real estate became a passion in my life. I started slowly, and confidence began to build as I had success. I loved listening to people and helping them as in the church. That was great training! My mother now lived with us because her sight deteriorated and she needed more assistance. I always went home to help her with lunch and prepare dinner, even a dessert.

Often contracts had to be signed with clients and I wouldn't want the family to wait on me for dinner. This was a bone of contention for Stuart. Dinner was cooked and in the oven, but he hated serving up the meal and he made it known!

We had to take turns calling our clients at night when they were accessible after work. In those days, we didn't have cell phones. Boldness grew in my life and I was making great commission and gaining sales. I had updated my vehicle several times with Stuart's help, but for the very first time in years I paid for the cars myself out of my own earnings. How wonderful that felt! After fourteen years of being a home-maker I was prospering and feeling so blessed! I gave all the praise to the Lord.

Chapter 4
God Was Leading

The call of God on our lives was as strong as ever. We knew to wait for His timing. After a couple of years of enjoying my work, and an ever-increasing work in the church alongside Stuart, there came this feeling of needing to move to Australia again. I always asked the Lord for confirmation as well as my husband's leading. This was an enormous step in our lives. It would involve me laying down my passion for real estate, which I struggled with in my mind, and even to this day has never left me.

I was still struggling with my speech. I had never forgotten hosting a visiting pastor for the church. He spoke a prophetic word over me. He said, "Colleen, God will heal you when you begin to preach." That was around the year 1975. This was quite frightening to me. Stuart had been careful to shield me, and here was this pastor saying the very thing that I feared. I never forgot it, but just put it away in the back of my mind.

Our children were growing and in school. Alan was finishing year ten; Raymon was in year eight; Little Sarah was in year four. This move was going to affect us all.

It was November 5th, 1984, and the move was on. The boys had finished college for the year and their master's had wished them well with the impending move to Australia, but we hadn't sold our home yet. The market was not good, so many things were against it.

I had left work in order to present my home for the sale and my boss was handling it. There were many negatives regarding the sale of our house. It was on a busy road and a corner block. Houses weren't selling and the market was depressed.

Stuart and I were having a discussion in the kitchen, when he asked me, "When will the house have to be sold?"

I answered, "It would have to be a cash buyer and would have to be sold by November 30th for our plans to go ahead allowing the children to begin in the new term in January 1985."

Remember, this was November, 5th. Stuart grabbed a large red felt marker and put a big ring around November 30th and wrote: "House Sold!" It was very ugly on my clean calendar, and my eyes kept getting drawn to it! Everyone who came to our home would see it. "How do you know this is not presumption?" I retorted. This was scary stuff!

He was not worried in the least! In fact, he even marked his calendar in his office in the same manner. Only putting, "HS", on that date. His fellow workers asked what that meant, and Stuart just replied, "Holy Spirit." They probably rolled their eyes, as that wouldn't mean very much to them! "God, this is your problem, and we are in faith!", we agreed.

Planning went ahead, and we decided to have a garage sale for November 30th. We had been trying to sell our three vehicles and advertised them regularly in the newspaper. There was very little response which was disappointing.

I had my car that I'd used for work, the boys had a little mini to run around in, and Stuart had another car as well. Over the years, Stuart had been very clever, restoring many vehicles. He did all the mechanical work, and spray painting and later sold them. This enabled us to renovate our home over the years. It was a lot of hard work, and he had a high standard with them all. This was tax-free money. Many a night I would spend time in the garage, handing him tools as he worked in the pit. At one time, he was painting tractors for the Ford Motor Company, and it was my job to blacken all the tires after the painting had been completed. When the boys were little, this was precious time together while they slept.

Before moving to Australia, Stuart made a quick trip over to talk with Pastor Neil Miers. Pastor Clark Taylor pioneered Christian Outreach Centre in Brisbane in 1974, and churches were being planted in many cities. Pastor Neil was happy for us to come, but said, "No promises." Stuart was happy for that to be the case and looked at schools for the family. In New Zealand, I was praying for him daily and seeking His guidance. The Lord gave me two definite Rhema Words:

One from Psalms 66:10-12 which read:

> *"For you Oh God, have tested us.*
> *You have refined us as silver is refined.*
> *You brought us into the net.*
> *You have laid affliction on our backs. You have*
> *caused men to ride over our heads; We went*
> *through fire and through water.*

*But you brought us out into rich fulfillment." (Some
versions say, "a wealthy place.")*

The second one was from Isaiah 46:11:

*"Calling a bird of prey from the east
The man who executes my council from a far coun-
try.
Indeed, I have spoken it.
I will also bring it to pass.
I have purposed it.
And I will also do it."*

We received great reassurance from these scriptures, especially me. The Lord was showing me that we were walking in
His plan. God had been guiding us through it all, and He was
in control. He had caused men to ride over our heads! I was
set free in my mind and could let all these concerns go!

Chapter 5
Farewell New Zealand

On November 25th, my boss brought a few men through our home for an inspection. They were from the Wanganui Veterinary Club, and yes, they were cash buyers! All the negatives (busy corner, too much traffic etc.) God turned to positives, and were just what they wanted! We were over-the-moon with excitement and praising God for the miracle! And there were more miracles to come!

November 30th came and what a busy day! People began to pour into our garage. One man asked us about the mini we had for sale. "Please hold it for me while I go to the bank.", he said. Another asked about my work vehicle. He said, "I've been looking everywhere for a car like this." I felt like saying, "Don't you read the newspapers?"

Then, Stuart was called into work where he had his other car on the car lot. The salesman said, "Someone wants to buy your car!" In two hours, three cars were sold! Another miracle!

Sometimes, it's the little things that one remembers so well. The following day, I had a knock at the door. The lady told me it was her daughter's birthday and she wanted to buy a citrus juicer to go on her kitchen whizz. She couldn't find one anywhere, but was inquiring if I had one? "That's strange", I thought. "How would she know to come to me?" I had never seen her before.

The incredible thing was, I had a brand-new juicer still in its box, that I had never used, and it was in the cupboard. Only God would know this. Yes, I sold it to her, and she went off happily to give it to her daughter. So random and so strange, but I felt the Lord was reassuring me that this was all in His will, and that He was confirming with signs following.

One of the hardest things I have ever had to do, was assisting mother to move and live with my older sister and family in Auckland. Mother was now blind having glaucoma and she needed assistance more and more. We never heard any negative words from Mum. She was bright and happy and was lovely to be around. I loved her dearly, as did Stuart and the children, so this was a great sacrifice for us all.

My family never totally understood why we had to move to Australia and they blamed the church for not using Stuart as a pastor. We never divulged that the senior pastor had forced Stuart to sign a letter requesting he was not to be called pastor. Stuart never cared about it, but I was upset that he willingly signed the letter. The congregation approached us on many occasions and voiced their objection to this, and said, "You are our pastor, and we will call you as such." We never spoke against our leadership but supported them over those twelve years.

Parting with treasures from a lifetime in my possession was so hard. I had won many book prizes from Sunday School, and my piano accordion, and all the music I had learned. Stuart had insisted we could not take it. With many tears and regrets, I had to let go. All sacrifice is difficult, and there is a price to pay. Maybe this was mine, along with my family and friends, and all that I held dear.

God provided help all along the way. We shipped a container to Australia and moved from our home to temporarily stay in a complete stranger's home, which one of my friends had arranged. It was amazing how He provided.

We struggled saying goodbye to our many dear friends, and prepared to enter a country to start a new life in Australia. Even the Ford Motor Company helped us with a car to drive to Wellington for the flight.

We were excited about our adventure and even the family embraced it with us. Our children were optimistic, and happy. We flew on January 3rd, 1985 from Wellington to Brisbane, but I was alarmed when the airline staff said we would have to pay $400 for excess luggage. I prayed silently as Stuart spoke with the staff and the Lord worked another miracle. It was okay!

Chapter 6
Arrival in Australia

We finally arrived in Australia on January 3rd, 1985 with bulging suitcases and feeling weary. The mental exhaustion was the hardest. Our move was monumental. Stuart's sister, Jacqui and husband Christian, were there to meet us. Also, a niece's husband with an extra car came to help us with our luggage and take us to the farm in Canungra, where they lived. It was good to be with family and know that we were not totally alone. The next morning, we awoke to find a snake slithering on the veranda and a wallaby nibbling grass below. We had arrived. The next move was to buy a car.

The New Zealand Prime Minister, David Lange had devalued the dollar, and overnight we lost $35,000 of our savings and house capital which was a tough blow! People said to us, "Maybe you shouldn't be going."

We answered, "If it's God's plan then we will trust in the Lord, and not in the mighty dollar."

Australia was an exciting place for us all. We loved Pastor Neil Mier's dynamic church in Nambour. We quickly adapted to Aussie life and patiently waited for our container of furniture to arrive. It took three months because of labor strikes on the wharf. We managed with the help of friends from church for beds, linen and secondhand furniture.

It was extremely difficult for our son Alan in a very different school system. I was so proud of how the family adjusted and coped with the many pressures in everyday life. Alan worked very hard in eleventh grade and with much determination he quickly caught up with work he had never tackled before. That year he won a Burnside Award for overall excellence, which was only one of ten awards given out at the end of the school year.

Stuart was invited to attend Ministry School in Christian Outreach Centre in Brisbane with Pastor Clark Taylor, and from there to go and pioneer a church with the family. Yes, just our family and a determination to plant a church for the kingdom of God to touch many lives. This was another scary step of faith! We had an overhead projector and Raymon had been learning guitar. Stuart would preach. The Holy Spirit said to me, "You'll lead worship."

"That would be a miracle!", I thought.

Stuart had totally released me of any pressure to preach or speak on the platform. He shielded me because of my struggle with speaking, so I had felt very protected and safe. Now this was something else, and it was the Lord nudging me forward. We started by visiting the area and looking for a house. Everything was too expensive for us, and even when the realtor contacted us to view a property, it was horrible and stunk. I remember saying to him, "Have you got a property that someone is desperate to sell?"

He thought for a moment, and hesitantly said yes. But followed by saying, "You'll never buy a house for $55,000." That was all we had, which included a $15,000 loan from the bank. We had previously approached our bank to secure a loan.

We drove to the property and instantly knew, this was the one. A three bedroom home, only two years old, with potential. The couple was selling for $65,000 but they were in a tough bind and needed the money. We returned to our vehicle, and with the $80 we had in our wallet, we signed a contract. The realtor said, "They may rip this contract up, but I will present it to the owners." Another miracle, and we had bought a house! We had a home to go to at last.

We pioneered our very first church in Tweed Heads, just over the border into New South Wales in 1986. Unfortunately, New South Wales had daylight saving, and Queensland didn't. We had two clocks in our kitchen. One on New South Wales time, and one on Queensland time!

Alan stayed in Nambour to finish his 12th Grade year with friends. With just Raymon and Sarah we planted the church and had our very first services in Tweed River High School Auditorium in 1986. We knew no one! We were on the water again, believing God. We laugh now when we recollect our early beginnings.

Our very first service, we had two ladies in attendance. I led the songs; Ray played his guitar; Sarah worked the overhead for the songs, and Stuart preached. One lady said her husband dropped her off for church while he went fishing. She said, "I'll just slip into the back row, and no one will notice me."

How funny that was to us when the service was over. The other elderly lady said, "I'm so glad you're starting a church here. I can't stand Pentecostal Churches!" We drove downtown, bought ourselves an ice cream and laughed!

That was our very first service. We had an offering of $63. We had put in $60 and the ladies $3.

The second service we had 4 people come. Now this was exciting. Two ladies gave their hearts to the Lord that morning. One of them has been our dearest friend, Nan Bower. She has just recently graduated to heaven at the age of 91 years. We shared many happy years with her.

One of our pastor friends from another city phoned to see how things went. Stuart told him we had a 100% increase that Sunday with four in our congregation. They both laughed. We had certainly begun and after a year we had a great church of mixed ages, from young families to the elderly. God was moving mightily in Tweed Heads!

Chapter 7
Pioneering Our First Church

In 1989, we had a prophetess from Texas come to Australia. We were encouraged to have her come to our church. The facility for our church was large, and had previously been an indoor cricket facility, which Stuart had visited with one of our elders. They loved the building, but at that time the business was booming.

We were to lease this building, in later years, and transformed it into a wonderful church in which we hosted other churches to come when we had special speakers. Cynthia Alexander, the prophetess, was one of these speakers. I drove to pick Cynthia up from her previous church and bring her to the Gold Coast. I felt very nervous. I had an old vehicle that Stuart was restoring, and was wishing I had a nicer vehicle to travel in. Very humbling indeed.

Cynthia's first request was, "Let's go and get ourselves a decent steak. I'm starving for one. The treat is on me!" So that's just what we did, and enjoyed it all. It was a good ice breaker.

We had a powerful night with many of our fellow pastors in attendance. Of course, there is always great excitement when a prophet comes to church. Everyone wants a word from the Lord. I remember standing in the prayer line with Stuart as Cynthia ministered to all the pastors who were called to the platform. We never had cell phones to record, but I remember her words clearly. "I see you going to America and ministering!" she told us.

How exciting that sounded, but we had waited on God's timing before, so we were going to just put this on the shelf, so to speak. However, one of our local pastors had been to America and often had pastors from there minister for him. He approached Stuart and said, "I can put you in contact with them and they will have you come."

Stuart said, "No thank you. If it's God, then He will cause it to happen."

We developed a great church of prayer warriors over the seven years there. Our people embraced the church and were keen to see the kingdom of God grow. The Lord was beginning to speak to us about getting ready to travel. Stuart had a piece of paper that he had written on when he was in prayer one day. It spoke of change and he wasn't game to share it with me. Change was always hard, and these folk were family to us. He knew I would take it badly. He kept it hidden for seven months and told the Lord, "You will have to prepare Colleen for this change."

One night, as we lay talking on our bed, I began to share with Stuart exactly what I was feeling. He said, "Wait, I have something to read to you", and retrieved the bit of paper he had hidden in his drawer. It said, "God is getting you ready for travel." It confirmed what I was feeling.

I came home from a Ladies' meeting one day, and one of our faithful congregation prophesied all that we had discussed on our bed that night. The Holy Spirit was speaking of change coming and had let it out. The cat was out of the bag!

Stuart also received a call from another lady saying she had a word of prophecy that revealed change was about to happen. It was true! We began to prepare for a replacement pastor. And so, after seven years, we stepped down from the church although we remained close friends within the congregation.

We decided to sell our home without a realtor and had a "For Sale" sign out front. It was Christmas time, and our very first lady buyer came to view it. She said, "If it's still for sale when I return from Sydney, I might come and buy it." That was exactly what she did.

However, she came to the home twelve times in all, and asked if I would make her a coffee, which I was happy to do so. She loved the atmosphere and was going through a separation from her husband. She just found it so peaceful in our home. This was all very well, but difficult bringing this sale to a close, especially because it was our own home.

One day, Stuart was going off to see a golf competition with Alan, and he gave me instructions; "If this lady comes again, close the sale!" I was under pressure.

Sure enough, she called in again, and then I spotted two ladies stop by our house to read the sign. The Lord was giving me a marvelous opportunity here. I excused myself for a moment and talked with the ladies in the parked car. Yes, they were interested in buying. I quickly walked back inside to share this with my buyer. "If you're not buying, I would like to bring these ladies through."

My buyer said, "Yes, I am. Please let me go to the bank to get a deposit, and I'll return with the money."

We prepared to move. I had felt a very definite check in my spirit about looking for a rental property.

A conversation happened with a friend who owned a large Caravan Park at Tweed Heads. Kay, who was in our congregation, began to tell me that they had bought another home and had moved from the manager's residence of the Colonial Caravan Park.

I wanted to cautiously approach the idea of renting her home but knew that her husband Barry was not a fan of ours, as he hated Christians. Not wanting to cause strife in Kay's household, I asked her to approach Barry for us, but if there were any angry words, just to let it drop.

Kay called me to say that Barry wanted us to come and talk with him. We met with Barry, who was very amicable, and he said, "There's one condition. You live here rent free, pay no utilities or phone, and when the office closes at 5:00 pm every night, you take over the bookings." Yes, this sounded perfect! To live in a big home with a pool out front, over the road from the beautiful inlet that was Tweed Heads with boats on the water and pelicans swimming nearby... what more could we want! The office was attached to the home, and I loved doing that type of work.

Stuart had resigned from the church, and was offered a job as groundsman, so we had an income and very little expenses to cover. God was providing for our family!

We were very happy in this home. But when we learned that the caravan park, with over 100 permanent vans and holiday cabins had been sold, we were concerned. "Lord, where does that leave us? Surely another owner would require the house to live in for themselves", I questioned the Lord.

I should have known all would be well. "Be anxious for nothing.", I reminded myself.

The new owners were elderly, and the manager they appointed did not need a home, as he lived nearby. The new manager was a wonderful man and became a dear friend of ours. Jane was the assistant manager. She had previously lived with us in our home with the family for eighteen months.

When it came time for us to leave the park, we had made many friends there. I remember a letter that Len, the Manager, wrote to Stuart. Stuart wept as he read Len's loving letter that said he valued Stuart's friendship and mate-ship, never having had that before. Every step of our walk, our love-ties with people were so strong, and it was difficult to leave.

A weekly prayer team formed of 24 committed prayers, and as we began to travel, they supported us in prayer. With a small pop top caravan (travel trailer) we traveled through Christian Outreach Centers in Queensland over the next six months. Some churches we stayed for a week, doing church services, ladies meetings, youth and school meetings. It was a wonderful time! Exhausted, and with all our energy spent, we would move on to the next church and do it all over again. We were self-sufficient, and paid our own way, just receiving a love offering.

On arrival in Rockhampton, we were told we were welcome to attend a gathering of pastors, and that Steve Shultz was ministering from America. Both Stuart and I will never forget this meeting.

We received this prophetic word from Steve (who later wrote "The Elijah List" on the internet):

> *"You are pioneers with a pioneering spirit, on a covered wagon and the Indians are coming up behind. But God says, don't worry, I am your rear guard."*

Wow. That blew us away! It was strange how the Lord was using this terminology. We don't have covered wagons in Australia, nor do we have Indians, but I had been brought up with my Dad taking us to the movies to see many Westerns. Dad loved them! So, from then on, our prayer team called us "Covered Wagon Ministries." Jane even designed us a card showing the covered wagon. We called our caravan "The Covered Wagon."

Wit our itinerary almost completed, we knew we had to visit the head pastor in Brisbane as we drove north to do our last lot of meetings. We made an appointment to see Pastor David. As soon as we were seated in his office and he had greeted us, he seemed to have a lightbulb moment. He said, "I need you to go down to the Central Coast, to take over a broken church. We need a Senior Pastor there." The previous pastor had left the church and taken nearly all the congregation with him.

The strange thing was, we knew the couple involved as they had attended ministry school along with Stuart. "Will you go?", he inquired.

Stuart asked for time to pray about it. There was a small group of faithful folk. But there was little else.

As soon as we prayed about this, the Holy Spirit confirmed it was of Him. We were challenged to go to a location close to Sydney and far away from family, who were married and living on the Gold Coast. We committed to go for six months.

We parked our caravan beside the small hall that had been for Youth and had to use the bathroom facilities. Cockroaches scurried across the floor as I made my way to the toilet at night. How revolting! I'd faced many challenges before, and this was a new one. Little did we know we would stay there eight years!

Chapter 8
God Has a Plan

The Central Coast was a fresh challenge for us, and we would encounter many things that we had not previously faced. It was very different compared to the other areas we had lived in, and there was more opposition in the demonic realm.

Friends from the Gold Coast came down to join us and work alongside. Our daughter Sarah, her husband, and our baby grandson, moved south, to be near us. We also welcomed Peter, Leonie McNab, and Jane Tyack from the Gold Coast.

It was not easy re-establishing, but we put our hand to the plough and didn't look back. There were many under-currents in the church as we tried to take the reins. Gradually, things settled down. We developed some very good leadership and young families became involved. It was a great congregation, with a good team of support for us as pastors. Stuart was made Area Chairman, with several churches under his wing. The New South Wales Chairman had him teach in Newcastle each week at the Bible College. This was a big commitment.

Prayer played a big part in our lives. One night, after a very positive and powerful leadership meeting in our home, Stuart had a dream. It was a night vision, I believe. We had gone to bed about midnight, and both dropped into a sound sleep. Stuart recounted the vision to me the next morning. He felt he was positioned in a large armchair, with his feet stretched out in front of him, and that he was flying.

There was a house in the distance and as he was approaching at great speed, he just went right through the house, like it wasn't even there. "*Weeeeee!*" He was flying over land and this air travel was very exciting! He travelled for quite some time, and suddenly, looking ahead, he could see a massive row of pine trees. He was advancing at a great speed. He swung his legs to the side, being fearful of smashing his limbs, and flew straight through the trees with no difficulty at all.

Traveling over land and water for some time, he arrived at a marketplace. He could smell coffee, and gazed through a trellis where couples were enjoying coffee and chatting. Others were strolling hand in hand, looking at shop windows.

He was standing on a cobbled path, and there was a large prominent door in front of him. On the steps to the door, stood a man, derelict and dirty, holding a little boy in his arms. The man made eye contact and held up the child in his arms. Stuart suspected the child to be about six years old. Stuart took the child in his arms and walked around for a few moments holding the child, asking the Holy Spirit, "What do you want me to do?"

In an instant, Stuart was told to lay hands on the child and as he looked at the little boy's leg, he saw a large weeping infected sore. "Lay hands on him." he was prompted, but his instinct was to withdraw his hand. The whole leg was such a mess! At this command, he laid his hand on the leg, and immediately, the little boy cried out, "Jesus has healed me, Jesus has healed me!" Stuart returned the little boy to the man (possibly his father) and immediately, he woke up in bed. It was 3:00am.

He put his hand out to see if I was there, thinking maybe he had died, but no, he hadn't. His skin was feeling like he'd had little cuts all over and it burned, but when he touched it felt quite cool. I was sound asleep beside him. It was now 4:00 am and he could wait no longer, waking me up to tell me what had happened.

We have never forgotten this vision, and it stays with us, even today. Something changed in Stuart's life from this time on. He had such a heart of compassion for those hurting, and even when he watched something very sad on TV, he would weep. We felt that the Lord was telling us some things concerning the vision. Obstacles would not be a concern; we would sail right through them. God had a plan and we just had to trust Him!

A healing ministry would always be a big part of our lives, and we would pray for many people.

Isaiah 1:19 says, "If you are willing and obedient, you shall eat the good of the land."

I found great strength from this verse. Yes, we were willing, and we would be obedient to the Lord!

Chapter 9
New Challenges

Life was good on the Central Coast, and the church was growing. We had a strong team and lots of young married couples with children. It was a healthy church. We had established ourselves there with a nice home and we loved serving in the community. We had great connections with local churches.

Our sons, Alan, Ray, and their families were living on the Gold Coast, so we loved it when we had the opportunity to visit and catch up with our grandchildren. It was here that our lives took another change.

One day, when Stuart was mowing the lawn in our small yard, the Holy Spirit spoke a word in his spirit. It was so strange, and so out of left-field that Stuart turned the mower off, before finishing the lawn, and came inside. I remember working in the kitchen when he came in and asked me, "Have you heard of Arkansaw?"

I thought for a moment, and said, "I think it's in North America." We tried looking on a map, but my next question was, "Why?" He said, "I heard it in the Spirit."

Stuart called the local travel agent and inquired, "Can you tell me where it is and how would I get there?" The young lady was gone for quite some time, and came back, apologetically, to the phone and said, "I'm sorry sir, we don't know." Oh dear, that wasn't much help!

Stuart called our Assistant Pastor, Peter McNab. "Peter, have you heard of Arkansaw?"

Peter said, "Yes I have. It's in America in the south." and he explained where it was. He said, "You're probably spelling it wrong. It's Arkansa**s**." Oh yes, Peter was right! How funny!

We found it on the map, with Little Rock being it's capital. We laughed about that one. "Well I'm not too sure what that is about." said Stuart, "But if it's God, then it won't go away."

Things changed in our lives from that very moment in March 1999. We researched all about Arkansas on the computer and anything we could lay our hands on. It became a passion and the more we learned, the more we felt called to pray for people in Arkansas. Stuart loved searching out Arkansas statistics.

Stuart had precious memories of life on the farm at Okoia and had memories of Dad playing the record of *Old Man River*. Stuart loved that song and I think he must have listened so much with Dad that he knew all the words by heart. There had always been a link to the Mississippi River. I remember him quoting all the statistics of the Mississippi River and bringing it into a sermon in our early years at Tweed Heads. It had even stayed with me to the same degree, but we had no idea of what the Lord was up to.

I remember Stuart preaching, "What makes it a great river, is what flows into it. Forty major rivers flow into it, and some 250 smaller tributaries." He likened it to our own lives, "What makes us great, in the Lord, is what flows into us:

Salvation, Baptism of the Holy Spirit, and Water Baptism. All of heaven flowing into our lives, makes us the people of God who we are today."

I so loved a Rhema Word the Lord had given to me before leaving New Zealand out of Jeremiah 29:11-14a:

> *"For I know the thoughts that I think toward you, says the Lord.*
>
> *Thoughts of peace and not of evil, to give you a future and a hope. Then you will call upon Me, and I will listen to you.*
>
> *And you will seek Me and find Me, when you search for me, with all your heart. I will be found by you...."*

This verse had given me such reassurance of God leading us and guiding at the time of moving overseas to Australia. It resonated within me over and over at times when I needed His reassurance and strength. We don't always understand what the Father is directing us to do, but we trust that He knows the beginning and the end and has it all in hand.

Our prayer meetings grew and took a powerful turn for the better. Sometimes, we had people from other churches attend and had 75 regular prayers. Stuart decided we would have a Tuesday all-day prayer. People came as they could during the day. The focus was on the State of Arkansas. We had a huge world map pasted on the wall and had a red ribbon from our location in Australia, stretching across the world to Little Rock, Arkansas. It was spectacular, and eye catching, and we often prayed, focusing on that red ribbon.

We felt we were connecting with prayers of intercessors in Arkansas. We were praying for a state we did not know, and a people we did not know, but there was such love going out towards them. Visitors to our church asked what the red ribbon represented, and we told them how we had begun to pray for Arkansas.

The enthusiasm for this state in America grew, and I shared with many ladies' groups as the passion took hold. I began to get invitations to go and speak in other churches of Christian Outreach about what God was doing. However, I did this with fear and trepidation because I still struggled with a stammer. But I did this in obedience to the Lord. The more enthusiastic I became, the bolder I could speak, and joy took over. All our friends in Christian Outreach knew of our passion in prayer.

During the year of 1999, we took a team from our church on a mission trip to Fiji, in the Pacific. I was not planning to go on this trip, but as one of our members was unable to go that made up the numbers, I decided to accompany Stuart after all.

We were part of a large team going to many islands which made up the Fijian archipelago. It was wonderful ministering to these happy people who had so little, but their love for the Lord was strong. We stayed with pastors in the villages and when we prayed for these precious people, God came through in Power. The Lord had told us back in the 90's, "Get ready for travel." and we were doing it.

We attended our main Conference for Christian Outreach in Brisbane and took a team of our leadership to attend the

Conference with us. These were gatherings of around 3,000 people, and worship and ministry were top notch. The meetings were very long, anointed, and life changing. We were so excited to be there!

At one point, there was an altar call for people wanting to step into their destiny. Stuart and I looked at one another and agreed. "Let's go!"

I was in my own little bubble of receiving from the Lord, when I glanced around, looking for Stuart. He had gone back to his seat. "That was strange." I thought.

I returned to my seat, not understanding exactly what had taken place. "Stuart, what happened?" He said he felt reprimanded by the Lord, "I've given you a destiny already! Arkansas."

"Yes, I'm sorry Lord." he repented quickly. Oops, it's not nice when that happens; when we step out of line!

In that very same Conference, with all the singing and worship going on, the Lord gave Stuart a vision. It was the hub of a wheel over Little Rock, and the wheel was covering the whole state. He could see spokes going out from the hub, some reaching into other states of America, and some short over Arkansas. At the end of these spokes, were blobs. He asked the Lord, what are these, and the Lord replied, "These are churches that I will move in by my Spirit. The churches that won't allow the moving of the Spirit, I will bypass."

Stuart heard the Lord say, "It will not be one church, or one denomination. It will be over the whole state of Arkansas, and no one will be able to take credit for it, as it will be a mighty Revival, and moving of the Holy Spirit. Many prodigals will return to the Lord, and churches will be full to over-flowing." This is the message that we carried for Arkansas.

Chapter 10
A Step of Faith

We continued to pray for Arkansas, and were feeling more and more that we had to take a step of faith in order to go. The only thing we could do to raise the finances would be to sell our home. We prepared our home, and engaged a realtor. We were believing for it to sell, but nothing happened over a four month period. It was like the Lord was resisting the sale. I said to Stuart, that I felt God was wanting us to trust Him, and believe Him for the finances. We both decided to do this, with encouragement from our Assistant Pastor, Peter.

With a plan in our minds, we visited a travel agent and booked a ticket from Sydney to Los Angeles. Next, onto Dallas/Fort Worth, and then we would travel by Greyhound bus to Little Rock. We needed some insurance, and I remember the trip was going to be $8,500 in total. We put a deposit of $100 down, and were not sure where the rest was going to come from. We were on the water again.

I remember confiding in Stuart that I felt like a fraud as I walked out of the travel office. We booked our flight for March 12th, 2000 and planned to stay for a month. After a year of prayer, it was time for action!

Our church was excited and we were believing for God's provision for God's plan. We just asked the church to believe with us, and had a goal in mind of $10,000. The Lord provided $12,500 in all, and I remember exchanging $10,000 and finishing up with $5,000 US dollars. Our credit card was for back up.

Three weeks before we were booked to leave Australia we had a regional Conference for New South Wales, which was our state. We had to attend before it actually started because Stuart was an Area Chairman. Other leaders were gathered and one of our friends said, "When do you go to Arkansas?" I replied, "In three weeks."

A friend, Sandra, was startled when I spoke "Arkansas", and asked again, "Where?" She said, "My husband, Burrell, had a vision of Arkansas five years ago!" We couldn't believe what we were hearing. We rushed over to Pastor Burrell to hear his story, with ears and eyes wide open. What was God up to?

My mind flashed back to a comment Stuart had made in the early stages of praying. He said, "Lord, I'm too busy, send someone else." The Holy Spirit replied, "I have asked others and they won't go!"

"Wow, I'll never say that again." Stuart confessed to me. Of course, one has this thought of others, somewhere in the world saying that, but never of a friend of ours, and a man in Christian Outreach Centre.

Pastor Burrell Glasspell told us his story. Five years previously, he was praying for a man who was about to get married. As he prayed, he saw an open vision, and saw the map of the state of Arkansas. He knew it was Arkansas because the name was under the map. As he watched the vision, he saw the Blood of Jesus flow down from the top of the state, and cover the whole of Arkansas.

Tears began to flow from our eyes, as Burrell and Sandra recalled the vision. We could hardly believe what the Lord was doing. Burrell went on to tell us what happened afterwards. He made plans to talk with a preacher in Sydney, Pastor Jack, who was from America, and tell him his vision.

Pastor Jack said, "Nobody goes to Arkansas! Toad Suck Arkansas!" It killed the vision inside of Burrell, and he did nothing more about Arkansas, but never forgot what the Lord had shown him. We all wept. He said, "I wish I was coming with you!" What an amazing thing; to have someone we knew well, who originally had that passion for a state like we had, and then to have it robbed from him just as quickly as it came.

There was also another exciting thing about Conference. We had a visiting Australian pastor that we knew well, who had been living in Denver Colorado. He was the guest speaker for our Conference. After he ministered, we went to speak with him. He was the American Chairman and we wanted to submit to him, and tell him what we were going to be doing.

After telling him about the vision and how we had believed God, he proceeded to tell us, "No one will have you to preach, Stuart; You're unknown. The American people are lovely people. They will take you out for a meal, but no one will take you to their home."

There was certainly no encouragement there! As we walked away, I said to Stuart, "Do not receive that word! Someone is going to take us to their home." I felt certain of it! We wouldn't let any negative words rob from what we believed. Our year of believing God for Arkansas had strengthened our resolve!

I remembered the words of our pastor friend, Ian, telling me, "Colleen, this is no small thing." We weren't too sure of anything, or had any concept of what God would do, but went in obedience to what we felt He was saying.

With one suit each in our luggage, we set off for America for the first time in our lives. We had never flown such long flights, and were ready to face the unknown.

ARKANSAS OR BUST!!!

FIRST ASSEMBLY OF GOD

North Little Rock, Arkansas

Our 50th Wedding Anniversary 2016

Chapter 11
On the Water

We reached LAX and had to retrieve our luggage and stay at a hotel overnight. Everything for the very first time is challenging. We felt excitement, and trepidation at the same time! Help! As I showered in the hotel, I felt the movement of the plane. It was a strange sensation indeed.

The next day, after a good meal and a bit of sleep, we set off for DFW. It was exciting! We were on a mission and heading to Arkansas! We stayed at another hotel in DFW, and from there we took a shuttle into Dallas. We looked at some historical places, like where President Kennedy was shot. I remember seeing it all on TV many years ago and it was amazing to be standing in that place reading the memorial monument. The next day, we planned to book seats on the Greyhound bus so we could see as much of Arkansas as we could, not really knowing what was in store.

The folks taking the bus all looked a bit dangerous, and I remember Stuart saying, "Keep your hand on your bag." One lady spoke to me and asked if we were missionaries. I smiled, and said, "Yes" because I felt like we were. When we reached Texarkana, Texas, the bus stopped and we got out to stretch our legs. I didn't see the step, rolled over on my ankle, really doing some damage, and doubled over in pain. I remember saying to Stuart, "Well nobody knows we're here, but devils do!" My ankle began to swell, and I had my legs hanging down for hours on our seven hour bus journey.

As we travelled through Arkansas we had our eyes glued to the windows. "Lord, we're here!", we said. The bus pulled into the bus station at what was then known as the ALLTEL Arena. Now this was scary. What do we do? Stuart said, "Let's sit on this seat and pray." Sounds good, but all he said was, "We're here Lord!" I went inside and tried to call some hotels but the money was an enigma to me. When I enquired whether the hotel had a shuttle, as they had done in Dallas, the clipped answer was "No ma'am."

I didn't know where to go from there. We decided to go over and speak with an elderly black taxi driver whose ash tray was overflowing. He kindly said, "I think I know where you would be safe. I can take you to Master's Inn downtown, Little Rock. What a good idea that seemed to us! We were here for the Master.

Stuart booked us a room for a week, on a cheap deal. This was not a plush place to stay, but we were grateful to be here in Little Rock after praying for a year. We opened the blinds on the sixth floor. There was the city of Little Rock stretched out before us, and a busy six-lane motorway at our feet. "Thank you, Lord." was our prayer. He'd said, "When you get there, you will meet people who will be instrumental in doing what I want you to do."

My ankle was now swollen, and black. The plan had been that we would walk and pray in Little Rock, and now I was unable to do that. Stuart rose early in the morning and navigated his way to find a crossing over the motorway. He walked and prayed, but never heard a word from the Lord.

We had a rental car booked at the airport to pick up, and Stuart gave me definite instructions that he needed to postpone this booking until he felt able to drive on these crazy roads, and on the wrong side of the road! The fast lanes were on the left, and the cars were traveling at full speed.

I had to try to converse with car hire assistants, and the only answer I was getting was "No ma'am". No one could help me, as they told me in no uncertain terms, that bookings made in Australia had to be altered by Australia, and of course I had no means to do that.

What a dilemma everything was. It was so hard. We had to take a taxi to the airport to retrieve the vehicle. Poor Stuart! We drove out on the roads and he made a beeline straight into a service station. We'd only just left the airport and he panicked, and felt unable to drive. After some deep breathing he returned to the car, and we headed to the hotel where we were staying. Everything was so hard, but we knew we had God with us, and this was His plan.

Daily, we would drive to the library, where we discovered that one could use a computer for one hour, free of charge. This was brilliant! Stuart got on one, and so together, we were emailing our family and our intercessors to tell them our news. It was a lifeline to us, and their comments were encouraging. How we longed to have that connection daily with our home base.

Seven days went by. We never heard from God. We witnessed to folk everywhere, and talked to many about what the Lord had shown us, about how we had prayed for one whole year for this state. Stuart asked the Lord, "Where should I go, Lord?" He said, "Everywhere you go I will bless. You can have the whole state."

What gems from the Lord we had received in Australia, but we were here **now**! We needed help **now**!

Chapter 12
"We Are Here, Lord"

One day as we walked down by the bus station there was a lady sitting in a parked car. Stuart said, "I'm going to talk with that lady." I said, "I'm not coming, she looks fierce." As he walked over to speak to her, he saw she had her Bible on her lap and she was reading it. She was waiting for her husband to have his hair cut. Stuart began to talk with her, and tell her our story. She said, "Don't give up or be discouraged. God knows we need you!" She said, "Go down to the radio station down the road, and preach over that." Now that seemed to be a great plan because the Holy Spirit had told Stuart he would preach over radio and television!

Now this was something that resonated in our spirit, so we set off to find this radio station, not knowing that it was a black radio station. The people were lovely, and we booked a half-hour slot each day for the following week. There would be plenty to talk about and at least we would be getting our story over the air waves. Nerve wracking yes, but we had to do it!

We had researched a large Assembly of God church in North Little Rock on-line and decided to attend the Sunday morning service. Daylight Saving time was starting on that same morning. Stuart set the alarm for us to attend. Unfortunately, he set it the wrong way, and we were an hour late. Oh dear!

Service was underway. We were ushered to a seat towards the back of this huge church. It was a large magnificent glass structure, of which I have never seen the like. The congregation was in worship and the gowned choir was singing. The presence of God was there. Stuart and I thought, "Surely, we will hear from the Lord here." We so enjoyed the preaching of the Word and afterwards met Pastor Garrison and others.

Someone must have passed him a note that some Australians were in his meeting. He welcomed us and asked us to stand to our feet.

After church, they invited us to come to the night meeting, but Stuart had the thought that he wanted to go to Pastor Happy Caldwell's church to see what was happening there. We were feeling desperate to hear directions from the Lord as this was now the eleventh day since we had arrived.

We negotiated the roads a little better, and found Pastor Caldwell's church. It was a great service and the presence of God was strong, but the Lord was not talking to Stuart. The church was very welcoming. As in the morning service, the pastor had us stand so they could welcome us. We stopped and ate at a restaurant, then returned to Master's Inn.

As we opened the door to our room, Stuart heard the Lord say, "This week I'll open it up! " Wow, that was so good! We were extremely excited about that and rejoicing, when, the phone rang. We looked at one another and thought, "Who's that?" No one knows us.

Stuart refused to answer it, and I certainly was not keen to either. I said, "You answer it." and he refused again! Oh dear,

I picked up the phone. It was a lady from Pastor Garrison's church, and she said, "Pastor Garrison was looking for you tonight. Where were you?" I replied, embarrassed, "We were at Pastor Caldwell's church." She proceeded to tell me that Pastor Garrison had asked, "Would someone please take those Australian's out for a meal?" She said, "I will!"

How Dorothy knew where we were staying baffled me. Someone on the door must have told her where we were staying. They were probably shocked, as we were on the wrong side of the highway, and the other hotels were all on the other side. It's strange how God had turned this together for our good.

The following morning, we had an appointment at the radio station to share our vision over the air waves. We were to meet Dorothy for the very first time at Olive Garden in North Little Rock for lunch. The radio time-slot went well. We got in the rental car, left the station, and pulled out onto a side-road to a stop sign. There was a busy four-lane road and it had been raining, so the ground was wet.

Without a word of a lie, we suddenly found ourselves pushed out onto the busy road, and to Stuart's left, a large black Ford F250 pickup was powering towards us.

The driver came to a sudden stop, too close to Stuart's door for comfort. We had been pushed out onto the road. The driver sat, shaking his head, as Stuart reversed back to the stop sign. I think I had my head in my hands. We were so shaken. There was no one behind us. This certainly was a spiritual attack and not bad driving on Stuart's part. The devil knew if he could wipe us out, we could make no more inroads into Arkansas. It was frightening.

Chapter 13
"Help, Lord!"

We met Dorothy and some other friends of hers at Olive Garden, and after only a few minutes with the group, Dorothy offered to have us come to stay in her home. I began to cry as she went on talking, and she asked why. I think that after the near accident, and the confirmation of being asked to come and stay at her home, everything had caught up with me. What I had felt the Lord would do, He did. God was in control!

After lunch, Dorothy made a phone call to another lady, Ruth Finley. We learned Ruth had just connected all the intercessors of Arkansas on the internet. It's amazing how God works! We had been praying for intercessors in this state, and now we meet with Dorothy, who happened to be the head intercessor for this large Assembly of God church with members in excess of 2,000.

That evening we met Ruth and we were all connected. Ruth visited Dorothy's home that afternoon and we shared our story. Tears flowed as we talked. Ruth planned to return home to send out a message to all the intercessors, telling how the Lord had sent us, and that we had a message from the Lord for intercessors of Arkansas.

Dorothy and Ruth had been praying for their state for many years for a move of God's Spirit, and now saw that two Australians had been sent as part of the answer. God was connecting the dots together, and suddenly we were thrust into something that was bigger than we could ever conceive, just by being willing and obedient.

Things were coming into place as they realized their prayers had not been in vain. We were sent by God, and they recognized it. There was great excitement and faith was exploding in our connections! These were the people the Lord had told us about. We didn't know how we would meet, but He was doing it.

We returned to Master's Inn to finish out our second week there. Then, at the end of that, we made plans for Dorothy to help us return the rental car, and we would stay in her home.

On that Tuesday, Dorothy invited us to an intercessor's meeting at the Assembly of God church. Of course, these folk were all strangers to us, but there was a connection in the Spirit realm that was so tangible. As we began to pray, it felt like we were instantly at home and there was a "oneness" in the room. I couldn't stop weeping as I prayed, and we just laid on the floor prostrate before the Lord.

God was truly in control, and there were no words for what was happening. The presence of the Lord was in the room, and suddenly we felt like we were with family. It was truly overwhelming! We shared a little at times, then these precious people began to wash our feet with tissues, and pray over us. The prayer meeting began at 10:00 am and continued throughout the day, with men and women coming and going till 6:00 pm that night.

Stuart prayed for many, prophesying over different ones. One man approached him and asked if he would take his class the next evening. He told us that over 1,000 people come to church on Wednesday nights for teaching in different classrooms. Stuart inquired what subject he was teaching, and he said "Holiness".

"Yes.", Stuart replied, knowing that he had this simple thought, "If anyone asked him to do something, he would say "Yes". We had come to Arkansas with that song, "Yes Lord, yes Lord, yes, yes, yes."

Wednesday night came and we were ushered into a room packed with about 100 people. We were given seats on the front row and we both felt nervous. The pastor that had invited us introduced Stuart, and just as he began to speak, a man entered the meeting a little late. The only available chair was the one Stuart had been sitting on.

I was a little embarrassed as the man spoke to me and sat down. Stuart was ministering on the Holy Spirit, and God was moving powerfully. I remember him talking about how the Lord revealed to him, in Australia, that we would be on radio and television. I remember wishing he hadn't said that in the meeting. "What if that never happens?", I thought to myself. Too late, it was out! Little did I know the next part of the story.

Chapter 14
Open Doors

This man Duane, had received an email from Ruth, as he was also part of the intercessors of Arkansas. Ruth had advertised the fact that we would be ministering at the Assembly that Wednesday night. Duane managed a TV Station in West Monroe, Louisiana, just over the Arkansas border. (The programs there aired in North Louisiana and South Arkansas) Now Duane lived 3 hours away and he knew that he didn't have the extra finances to drive that far.

In the afternoon, he had a knock on his door. The El Dorado Police Chief gave him an envelope and said, "The Lord told me to give you this!" God had supplied, and he was going to the meeting in Little Rock. Coincidence? Absolutely not! God was doing the connecting and things were happening fast. We later learned there were people that drove from Memphis to attend that meeting. Word had gotten out that God had sent us. After the meeting, Duane invited us to go on his TV program. The answer was, "Yes!" We have been on TV many times since then.

Things were moving at break-neck speed. Stuart was asked if we were available for a statewide gathering of intercessors on the next Saturday at the Assembly of God Church. They had planned this meeting, but didn't have a speaker. "Will you be our speaker?" they asked. Our answer was "Yes". Coincidence? No!

Thursday night we were asked to come to a church in Alexander, just out of Little Rock. The intercessor had spoken to her pastor. "Yes.", was our reply. Things were moving fast!

After a powerful meeting and hours of ministry, we returned to our hotel very late. After 7:00 pm security guards let us in. We hadn't realized all these details when we first arrived, but now we were fully aware. The carpark was locked and access in and out was monitored very closely. I think it was almost midnight when we got into bed.

Stuart had been asking the Lord what he should minister to the intercessors. He had been instructed by the Lord in Australia, "Don't take study notes, just your Bible." Just as he was asking and praying in the Spirit, the Lord began to tell him, "Tell the intercessors to be prepared and ready"

Whoa! He leapt out of bed, grabbing paper and pen. He motioned to me not to talk or interrupt him. He was busy writing furiously. The Lord gave him all the instructions of what to speak to the intercessors, including when to have me come and pray in the meeting at the Saturday event. He had Scriptures and all, in his 9 pages of notes.

This meeting was to go from 10:00 am till 4:00 pm in the afternoon, with a break for lunch. What a powerful day it was! The presence of the Lord was so strong, and Stuart spoke confidently from the notes that he had taken. He called me to come and pray at the appointed time, specified by the Holy Spirit.

I know I had never spoken so authoritatively and powerfully, ever before! The Power of God was in that meeting, the heavens were open, and His presence was so tangible. There was such a high level of faith and expectancy in the room. We prayed individually for all in the meeting. In the afternoon, someone came and told us that Pastor Garrison, the Senior Pastor, was in the meeting and taking notes as Stuart ministered. We prayed for him as he came in the prayer line, but of course we had little knowledge of who he was. It was a marvelous day, and we were happy knowing it had been part of His plan.

Chapter 15
Water Walking

Dorothy informed us that she had a call from Pastor Garrison, asking Stuart to minister on Sunday night in the church. She said we were to go and meet him in his office beforehand. This was quite nerve wracking as we learned he was a powerful man in the Assemblies of God, and would later become State Chairman. He was so welcoming to us, and not intimidating at all. In fact, he really opened his heart to us. We were ready for Sunday night, and we were told the details. It would be recorded for television, and Stuart would have one hour to minister.

Sunday night worship was awesome and we were both so nervous. I was praying for Stuart as he was called to the podium. A magnificent choir sang, adorned with robes and the presence of God was in the room. Pastor Garrison introduced Stuart, explaining that Stuart was a stranger to him. He explained that in 80 years, this was the first time, in the life of this church, that a stranger and a foreigner had preached in this church. But then Pastor Garrison went on to say that he felt he had to ask Stuart to minister.

The Holy Spirit instructed Stuart to do two things. First, he told the story of how the Lord had brought us to Arkansas, and about the vision that was given to him.

Then he began to challenge the men to allow the Holy Spirit to invade their lives and to stand to their feet, just where they were, to receive. He said, "Men who don't want this to happen, please don't stand." Men stood up all over the auditorium. Stuart began to pray, releasing the Holy Spirit to move.

All of a sudden, there was a cry that went out from the balconies, then all over the auditorium, as men began to cry so loudly, and they clung onto one another. It was a raw sound, and I have never experienced anything like it, as men began to cry out from their hearts to a Living God. He, the Holy Spirit, was invading their lives! God was truly doing something very powerful. Stuart just stayed silent waiting for the Lord's leading, not wanting to cut off what the Lord was doing. When things settled, the men sat down in their seats.

Then, it was time for the second thing the Holy Spirit instructed him to do. Stuart called for men and women whom medical science could do no more for their condition, and they needed a miracle, to please come forward and we would pray. The altar area filled with people and Stuart asked Pastor Garrison if he would anoint all those who were coming with oil. Then he asked if we both could pray.

As people were flowing into the altar area Pastor Garrison said to Stuart, "I didn't know there were so many sick people in my church." Pastor Garrison anointed everyone, and we laid hands on them all. People were laying over the altar, and crying out, receiving their healing.

That was a night we will never forget! It is etched in our spirit and as we recount these memories it still burns in our souls. This was the reason the Lord sent us, which after 23 years, (at this writing) still burns in our lives. It's like we come alive when we recount the journey and the memories.

After this service, many ladies told us they wanted to respond as their husbands had, but it was for the men. Many things happened after that meeting. We were offered a camper van and a house to stay in, but Dorothy wanted us to stay with her. We were not fully aware of it all, as people were wanting to meet us, and chat. Our minds were in a whirl as there was so much happening and so very fast.

One of our intercessors, Debbie, wrote an encouraging email to us. These emails had been our lifeline for eleven days when we were going through the trial of our faith and we had to return to the library to access them.

Debbie reminded me how Stuart had been told in a prophetic word that he had a head like a diamond, and he was going to butt the kingdom of darkness with his head. She continued, "I see like a glass cocoon over you. Just tell Stuart to butt it with his head." I laughed when I read this. What a confirmation it was! North Little Rock Assembly of God was a magnificent glass structure, two stories high, and all that we did was walk through the front door. It explained it perfectly! Isn't God wonderful? We were seeing Him opening doors right in front of our eyes, and now we were meeting the very people He spoke of. Our days now became a whirl.

Dorothy had 40 calls on her phone daily from people from all over Arkansas, inquiring where we were going to be, and pastors, urged on by their intercessors, were wanting us to come to their Assemblies and minister.

They said, "If Pastor Garrison has had them, then we want them." Whereas, normally permission should be granted by the AG Headquarters. God had by-passed man's system. Our days were crammed full. We were driven to all four corners of the state, and sometimes from one city in the morning, to another at night.

We had thirteen days left, before we were returning to Australia, and we had nineteen meetings booked all over Arkansas. We literally ministered in the morning, and were driven to the next location, with Stuart preparing as he travelled in the back seat of the car. The Lord had said, "Wherever you go, I will bless. You can have the whole state."

These words were etched deep within us. They were coming alive in reality before our eyes. Our faith was strengthened. Holy Spirit's power was touching and delivering people, and healings were manifesting. Major healings were taking place, and most were unknown to us at this time. Many were filled with the Holy Spirit, with the evidence of speaking in tongues.

2 Timothy 1:6 &7
"Therefore, I remind you to stir up the gift of God which is in you through the laying on of my hands.

For God has not given us a spirit of fear, but of power and of love and a sound mind."

Chapter 16
There's More

Our homecoming was exciting, and our church was thrilled to have us home again. Never did I dream of what would come next. Later, that very first week, Stuart dropped a bombshell! He told me the Holy Spirit had said, "You have to go back. You're not finished in Arkansas."

That was a shock to me! "How can we possibly go back, when we've just come home? We have a great responsibility to the church. We can't possibly go back!", I said. Our Assistant Pastor, Peter, said, "You must go back. Don't worry about the church. I will take good care of it."

So that's just what we did. Stuart contacted both Ruth and Duane to discuss it with them. Stuart said we would return for 60 days, and they said, "Leave it with us." We were shocked to learn that within three days of our phone call, they had set up an Itinerary of 55 meetings. We had a month in our church, and then returned to Arkansas.

There was a lot of opposition that arose, even in our denomination from higher up. Attack was coming against what God was leading us to do, and we were going in a different direction to what leadership wanted. We made the choice to follow what the Lord was leading us to do, at the risk of being ostracized by our State Chairman.

The battle was great in the invisible realm. The opposition was very strong, and the cost to do so was enormous. I'm not referring to monetary cost, but the devil was not happy and we knew as much.

> *Ephesians 6:12*
> *"For we do not wrestle against flesh and blood, but against principalities and powers, against the rulers of darkness of this age, against spiritual hosts of wickedness in the heavenly places."*

> *1Peter 4:12*
> *"Beloved, do not think it strange concerning the fiery trial which is to try you, as though some strange thing happened to you."*

We returned for the second time, and ministered all throughout the state. Meetings went on for hours, and in many churches services went far into the night. The Holy Spirit was flowing, words of knowledge were so accurate, and many healings were taking place. People with injuries from accidents were pinpointed and miracle healings were happening. Hundreds of people were getting filled with the Holy Spirit and speaking in other tongues. Stuart ministered a lot on the Holy Spirit to bring people to a place to receive.

I remember an Assembly of God church in Malvern. The service finished late into the night. People asked whether the pastor would leave the church open after service (midnight), as they just wanted to sit in the presence of God. They had never experienced it like that before. Pastors were wanting to have fellowship with us before we moved on, so that meant we were eating at 12:30am. The only place we could go was to Waffle House. That was all that was open at such late hours. Stuart preferred not to eat before ministering, but I can tell you, I was so sick of a diet of Waffle House!

Friends made themselves available to pick us up from our motels and often we had very little sleep before moving onto another church. It was a very exciting time for us and the Holy Spirit told Stuart that He would sustain us! I'm not quite sure just how we managed to do it, but with strength from above, we did.

People ferried us from church to church. We stayed in pastor's homes and wherever He directed us, as per our schedule. The hospitality was amazing and so much was happening, unknown to us at the time. In retrospect, as we reflect on some of the things that happened, we are in awe at what the Lord did.

In our first trip, we went to De Queen Assembly of God. It was amazing how this came about. There were ladies from the De Queen Baptist Church that were very hungry for the things of the Spirit. I'm not sure of the finer details, but we later found out that Shelley had phoned the Assembly of God pastor and asked if we could come and minister in his church. She knew the Baptist pastor would not allow us to go to his church. His answer was yes, and so De Queen, a very small township, was on the itinerary.

We were driven to De Queen. Church had begun and the car park was full. A big sign said: "Welcome Pastor Stuart & Colleen Price from Sydney Australia." We were quickly ushered into the Pastor's Office where he told us of this amazing story.

He said, "Who knew you were coming?" We replied, "No one." He said, "A man told me you were coming from Australia, and that I should get you to come. You would be in great demand, and that it would be difficult to get on your schedule." He said, "I tried to find the man who talked to me, and even wrote it in my diary (showing us), but couldn't find who had spoken to me." We were in amazement! No one knew we were coming and we knew no one in Arkansas. Only God.

He went on to share, "As soon as Shelley called, I knew this was the contact, so I never hesitated saying, 'Yes'". He said, "It must have been an angel, that talked to me."

It was a very powerful meeting in De Queen and there was a very significant healing that took place. Although we vaguely heard a few things, we had it confirmed four years later when the lady involved came to a meeting and testified what had happened.

This young lady had been diagnosed with multiple sclerosis and had given up her job as a physiotherapist, as she was unable to work any longer. She was only about 27 years old. Stuart called out all of her symptoms and she told us she thought, "What have I got to lose by responding?" Stuart and I prayed, and the Lord healed her! This caused a great stir in the community.

Chapter 17
God Supplies

2 Corinthians 5:7
"For we walk by faith and not by sight."

Our whole walk was a walk of faith. Trusting our Father's leading all the way. We bought our own tickets and God supplied the necessary funds. At times, He supplied with these in abundance and He never let us down. While we had the church, we never took wages when we were overseas. We just believed God to supply.

I particularly remember the time when he spoke to Stuart, "What are you prepared to lay down in order to do what I want you to do in Arkansas?" What did we have to lay down? We sought for an answer. We had to lay our church down. I struggled with that.

Our love for the church was great and we felt we had just come into a really good place. The church was growing and doing well. Stuart was an Area Chairman and had oversight over other churches. He was busy teaching in the Bible College in Newcastle every week. Life was exciting, but here was change coming once again. I remember speaking about how the Lord wants us to be flexible, but I had no idea just how flexible. Now it was being put to the test.

We were in Arkansas in 2002, in Frenchport, and Stuart was preaching about believing for a vehicle that we could buy when we returned on our next trip. A man came and spoke with me after the meeting and gave me his card with his email address. His name was Joe and he lived in Missouri.

Joe said, "When you return, just contact me and I will look for a vehicle for you." What a tremendous blessing Joe has been! In fact, the whole Moore clan have become dear friends. Joe sorted out a vehicle, and in fact, he bought it, cleaned it up, serviced it ready for us when we returned to Arkansas via, St. Louis. Joe and Fran picked us up and took us to their home. Joe financed our vehicle and contributed. Over time, we paid him back. We never had any problems with that vehicle over many years. On our departure to Australia, Stuart covered it up and stored it till our return. God supplied!

I remember an incident in 1993, when we had begun to travel in Queensland with our caravan, visiting churches and ministering. One pastor had been chatting with Stuart and made a pact to ask God if he could have a lap top computer. After talking with Stuart he said, "Why don't we both pray and ask the Lord for a lap top computer?" Stuart agreed and they made plans to chat in the morning to hear one another's answers.

In the morning, he was keen to hear Stuart's answer. "Not yet." the Holy Spirit answered. They both got the same answer. One night nine years later, in 2001 in Alma, Arkansas, while staying with our friends, Pastor David and Loretta, we just held hands and prayed concerning a computer. We reckoned it was time. Stuart had researched which one he would buy when he had the funds.

The very next day, in the service at Alma, Pastor Bill stood up and said, "All night the Lord was telling me we need to buy Stuart and Colleen a lap top computer now." Other pastors said they would contribute, and the amazing thing was, they purchased the very brand that Stuart had decided he wanted. What an amazing God we serve!

People would ask us, "Have you been to Vegas, New York, or many other places?" The answer was, "No." It wasn't that we didn't want to visit these places, but our itinerary was full when we came and there was no time to spy out the land. We are not tourists, but people on a mission. On one particular trip, I'd been telling Stuart I would love to see the Smokey Mountains of Tennessee. If we could squeeze a trip in, before we began our Itinerary, that would be so great.

We planned a quick trip to Tennessee in 2004. I was so excited. We would visit Memphis, Nashville, and travel over the state towards the mountains. We made a booking at a hotel, and overnight it snowed on the mountains. It was quite an unexpected fall of snow, but I knew my God had particularly blessed us with this snow fall. We traveled into the mountains and stopped to play in the snow. Many others were also out playing with their children, having lots of fun making snowmen.

We really enjoyed our visit to the area, and after a couple of days, made our way back towards Arkansas. With nothing planned, we thought we would head to Paragould to stay at a motel where a church had placed us to stay previously. They had a restaurant at the motel. We knew our funds were very low, but if we put some expenses on our credit card, we could deal with it later. We ate dinner at the restaurant, and added it to our bill, also intending to do breakfast there as well. After a good rest that night, we headed to the restaurant for breakfast.

As we were being taken to a table, a man called out, "Prices, Prices! Come over here and join me for breakfast." Did we know this man? I certainly didn't remember, and Stuart was looking vague. He certainly knew us, so we graciously joined him. As we ate breakfast, he chatted about our previous visit to Paragould, and how he had attended the meeting, along with many other pastors.

I will never forget that morning. I still didn't remember that pastor, but as we were chatting, he said, "The Holy Spirit is telling me to write you a cheque." Out came his cheque book. It was for $200. He said, "It will help you with fuel." Nothing had been said about our lack of funds, and this was amazing. The Lord had truly prompted him.

When we all rose from the table, he asked if we were leaving now. We replied that we had to gather our things in our room. He walked out with us and called us over to the receptionist and said, "These people are my guests and I want to pay their bill." He not only paid for our breakfast, but our dinner the previous night, and our accommodation as well.

I think of that dear man, and pray blessings on him. I only wish I had written down his name, but I think I was shocked by his generosity. We drove off to the bank to cash the cheque, praising God and singing our heads off. God had truly supplied!

As we traveled on our way, we passed a little township called Flippin. We saw a US Bank sign and knew that our insurance on our vehicle was being deducted automatically. We'd better check and put some money in the bank. Would you believe it? I took $50 into the bank and asked the teller when the withdrawal would be made. "Today", she answered. The account needed that $50 today. God had truly supplied our needs! Thank you, Lord.

I remember another time, when Stuart and I were in Eureka Springs. We were heading off to the Pancake Place for breakfast. We would just hold hands and pray, thanking the Lord for His provision daily, as we drove.

The restaurant was very busy. We settled into a booth and ordered our breakfast. I requested, "A separate plate for our pancakes please. I don't like egg mixing with my pancakes." After breakfast, some ladies who were in the adjoining booth, rose and went to pay their bill. One of the ladies returned and came to our table. She said, "This might seem very strange, but who are you?" She said she had felt the presence of God as she sat in the adjoining booth.

We proceeded to tell her our story, of how we had prayed for a year before coming to Arkansas and told her we were sent by God, knowing not one person or one church in this state. The lady proceeded to take out her cheque book, and wrote a $100 cheque. Another blessing from the Lord! She said she would attend a meeting in El Dorado, as she was visiting from Louisiana, and we did meet her again later in our itinerary.

At one stage, Stuart was asking the Lord why we hadn't seen many saved. The Lord said, "I haven't sent you to the lost, but I've sent you to my people. Minister to the body of Christ." He has told us that we would cross streams, denominations and people groups, and that is exactly what the Lord has done.

Chapter 18
Prophecy

In 1985, when we arrived in Australia, we were at our very first church service in Pastor Neil's church in Nambour. Pastor Drummond Thom, formerly from Cape town Africa, was preaching. He had a prophetic word for us that very night. I still remember him saying, "You will meet people that will be like family."

Prophecy, January 1985:

"For the Lord would say to you, my brother. The steps of a good man are ordered by the Lord, for yes, even in your heart, you have said, even to your family, 'Let us see what the Lord would have for us. Let us see where the Lord would take us. Let's find out God's direction.' And as you have prayed in so many words and have said, 'We will go where the Lord wants us to go, and do what the Lord would have us to do.' So, the Lord would say to you, 'Even as you have purposed to go, this has been My desire, not yours. I have placed the desire within your heart,' says the Lord. 'For I would have your lives, even to be taken and used for my Glory.'

"For there shall be many, that shall come across your lives, that you will touch. And there shall be many who will touch your lives. For the Lord says, 'I shall manifest Myself in a new way, and a

greater depth, and a greater reality of My Word, and you and your family shall get to know Me, says the Lord. And there shall be those that shall come across your path, they shall be just like family. And you shall meet them and say, 'We thank the Lord that you have become our friends.'

"For the Lord would have you to know, 'Even I am the one that is preparing their hearts and I shall bless you,' says the Lord, 'Even as I have blessed you before. And know this', says the Lord, 'that everything that you put your hand to do, I am the God that blesses. And as you praise Me and thank Me, you shall even see things that you purposed to do in your heart come to pass. For My blessings shall be upon them, says the Lord.'"

This was applicable to Australia and I've pondered on it many times. I am also aware of it more so in Arkansas. God has given us people that have been like family. They've taken us into their home and their hearts.

Darlene and Jay have given us a home to return to over many years, and we know it was the Lord who made that possible. Unbeknownst to Jay, as he began building an extension on his garage, the Lord was involved in the planning.

We first met Darlene in our very first visit in the year 2000, when she offered to help Ruth transport us to where we were ministering. Darlene said, "When you return next year, our room might be ready, and you could stay there." Well, God had a plan alright!

Arkansas was not our idea. We've often thought about how two people from half way around the world would pin-point Arkansas. Every time we've cleared customs in Los Angeles, they have asked, "Why, Arkansas, there's nothing there?" We have always replied "There are beautiful people." Now, they say, "Are you visiting family?" We just say, "Yes."

All of this has been God's idea. He has a plan for Arkansas, a future and a hope and we are just a small cog in a big wheel. God dove-tails everything together. Over the years, we have met many that God has brought from other states, to live in Arkansas. One day, the Lord revealed to Stuart, that people would be greatly blessed in Arkansas. They have struggled elsewhere, but have been blessed in Arkansas, because God has blessed it.

I love that scripture in Jeremiah 29: 11-13

> *"I know the thoughts that I think towards you, says the Lord, thoughts of peace and not of evil to give you a future and a hope.*
>
> *Then you will call upon Me and go and pray to Me, and I will listen to you.*
>
> *And you will seek Me and find Me, when you search for me with all your heart."*

It's quite amazing when we look back over the years, just how God has worked. Plunging us into a family, with Jay often reminding us, "This is not a home for wayward preachers!"

Poor Jay, the idea was for us to stay in the room he was building at the rear of the garage, but God's plan was for us to stay in the house. Darlene was in a precarious position, and wondering why she had so readily offered us a place to stay. Ultimately, God was in control, but it didn't really seem like that, and we, on the other hand, were thanking God for His provision whilst in Australia.

It is God that has knit our hearts to this family since our very first visit in 2001. Stuart, having grown up on a farm, has loved helping Jay on the land, tending to the livestock, the chooks (chickens) and mowing the grass.

Now, Jay calls Stuart, the yard boy! We often laugh together about it. We've seen the family grow, especially the grand children of Darlene and Jay, and now another generation has begun. I remember Kaylynn from the age of two years old. As she was growing up playing with friends at Darlene's, she would say to her friends, "Keep out of Sturt and Clean's room, and don't go in Sturt and Clean's bathroom." (That must have been how she heard our names.)

Chapter 19
Further Afield

What an epic journey and a walk of faith this has been!

Ephesians 3:20
"Now to Him who is able to do exceedingly, abundantly above all that we ask or think, according to the power that works in us."

Our journey is not over. We have been sent by the Lord. Doors are still open, and more opening each visit. There are too many to mention, and each church has been important to us no matter the size of the congregation, or the offerings. We have never been focused on finance and have just gone where ever the door opened. The Holy Spirit talked to Stuart that we would return 20 times. Our next journey in 2024 will be our eighteenth visit. We had to cancel in 2020 due to restrictions with covid, which was disappointing.

The Holy Spirit said, "When you get there, you will meet people who will be instrumental in doing what I want to do in Arkansas." All we knew was that we had to get there!

It's so amazing when we think back to these commands from the Lord. God has used people like pastors and intercessors, Godly connections, and now established friends, as close as family. There are too many to mention individually, but we have grown to love and honor them all. Some have passed into their Heavenly home now.

Stuart has always majored in Words of Knowledge, which have been extremely accurate and we did hear a pastor tell us that a rather irate parishioner berated him for sharing personal details before the meeting. Of course nothing of the sort had happened!

I remember well, a service we had with Pastors Jerry and Jearaldean in Murfreesboro. We already had held several services and we were asked to stay for another night. Stuart was encouraging the congregation to "sing in the Spirit" and "take the worship to another level in the Holy Spirit."

The presence of God was so strong that night, and after the singing, we just basked in His presence. The silence was electric with the Holy Spirit. There were many youths there that night along with their parents, but not a sound was heard.

Stuart was not able to preach, and both pastors just lay prostrate on the altar. God was in the house and He was doing so much! People tip toed out quietly when they had to leave after 9:00pm. Pastor told us later that that meeting was spoken about for a very long time.

One time, when we were ministering in Frenchport Assembly of God, a lady was praying at the altar. When Stuart came to lay hands on her he asked, "Where is your husband?" Well, he soon found out, that was a big mistake! This normally sweet lady had an angry expression on her face and was far from happy. He proceeded to tell her, "Well, I see you married", which was another bad mistake by Stuart.

The following visit to the church, a couple came to speak to Stuart. The lady asked, "Do you remember me?" Stuart answered, "No." Then she proceeded to tell him about her reaction when he went to pray for her. "Oh yes.", he remembered. He had never forgotten.

The man beside her began to tell his story. Only that week, he had gone to the pastor and told him that he felt he was going to marry this particular lady. When Stuart had said, "I see you married." he felt like jumping up and saying, "Here I am!" Of course, he couldn't, and over a period of time, between our visits, they had fallen in love and were happily married. We have had many young couples meet up in our meetings. Now they have married and have their own families.

Couples who have desired to have a family have come to the altar, many of whom have been told there is nothing more doctors can do to enable them to have children. Now they have their own children. Pastor Duane brought a handkerchief for some pastors in Texas that had also been desiring a child. We prayed and Duane sent the handkerchief to the pastors. They now have 16 year-old twins, having received a double portion!

Stuart had heard the Holy Spirit tell him during our flight over in 2002 to pray for couples who were wanting children. There are many in Arkansas that bring their children to us and tell us they are the miracle children these couples were believing for.

We were at The Ridge on our last visit in 2023 when a lovely young lady came to tell us that she was one of those children, and is now 19 years old. What a joy to meet these miracles!

It has amazed us when we have traveled to churches out in the country, where one would not expect strong churches due to the scattered population. On a visit to an Assembly of God in Charleston, Stuart prophesied, "I see you buying a piece of land, on a busy highway, and building a church there." That was exactly what they did!

On our first visit, after the church was built, we drove down the highway toward Charleston, and there was a large sign in front of this beautiful new church structure, saying, "Welcome Stuart and Colleen Price from Australia." We could see it flashing from a long way off. What an incredible fulfillment of prophecy and faith on behalf of Pastor Terry, and the late Murna, to do it! It is called "Life Church." This is a church with a high level of faith.

Our map of Arkansas is marked all over with every city and town highlighted, showing where we have been. Some small places are hardly even readable on the map, but we know we have been there. There have been God encounters everywhere. I remember Stuart praying, "Where would you have me to go, Lord." He said, "Everywhere you go, I will bless."

Chapter 20
Mexico and Beyond

We have had many opportunities to go to many other places as well. We were asked to come to Mexico to do an Easter Convention. Many churches gathered and camped by a river bed near Linares. It was a long and tedious journey from Arkansas, and the team from Paragould were in vans. We travelled down through Texas and over the Mexican Border.

Upon arrival at our destination, out in the country, we were surrounded by countless tents, as folk arrived with their families. It looked like a tent city. Over a thousand people were gathered.

Meetings went for hours, with Stuart working with interpreters to minister, and the people were hungry. These people were not rich in material things, but hungry to receive from the Lord.

I remember praying into the early morning, as people came for prayer on the altar, under a large covering, with wooden benches for seating. Ladies, beautifully dressed, were happy to lay under His Glory on the grass and receive from the Lord. I wish I had been able to converse in Spanish with them all, but their love was evident, and we did communicate with love toward them.

This was not our only visit to Mexico. We flew down to Monterey, on another occasion to minister over a two week period, only to find we had been double booked. We barely had time to splash our faces with water and were rushed off to a marriage seminar, where folk were in the service waiting for us.

God was doing some amazing things in our meetings and the Holy Spirit was flowing throughout. We were invited into churches that seemed very Catholic. People were weeping and receiving from the Spirit. Their hunger was enormous!

We drove up to Wisconsin for a conference with pastors. Then we drove across America; through Minnesota, South Dakota, and onto Billings, Montana to meet with pastors there, and have a meeting on our return visit.

Fellowship with pastors was important as well as our ministry times, especially those who were isolated from other ministries. Our Pastor friends, Steve and Carmen invited us to come to Alberta, Canada to minister. The drive was a real adventure for us. With our Lexus SUV we headed over the Canadian border and north to our destination. Steve and Carmen had an exciting, vibrant church, and had just undertaken to buy a theatre and convert it into a church. They had a real heart for Haiti, and had adopted many children from there into their family.

Stuart went with Pastor Steve to Haiti and saw, firsthand, the poverty and desperation of these precious people. So poor, and with little hope, pastors walked on foot to their congregations. Stuart and Steve bought one young pastor a bike to help him reach his congregation, and to another Stuart gave his new shoes, as the young man had holes in his.

They visited an orphanage, where there were a brother and sister that Steve and Carmen were in the process of adopting and waiting for papers to be processed. The devastation wrecked by the hurricanes that had hit Haiti were dreadful, and many lives had been lost. It was a dangerous place, due to the devastation and poverty.

Our time in Canada was powerful and we ministered in all aspects of the church. Our time with the family was so precious, and I remember sitting up many nights talking with Carmen in our dressing gowns. Steve was an early riser and Carmen was a late-nighter. Night after night, we stayed up till the morning hours, talking.

Everywhere there was a hunger for the Lord, we ministered. Our desire to minister under the leading of the Holy Spirit and to be obedient to Him was our driving force. This has never diminished over fifty years of walking with the Lord. Seeing people set free, healed, and delivered has been our passion. Our hearts have been for the people, and we've had hearts to pastor.

Chapter 21
Home Again

In December of 2007, after living in Arkansas for two years, we returned to Australia and to our precious family. It had been such a sacrifice to be away from our family and our many grandchildren, and we felt like there was a new season for us. But we never ceased to pray and have a heart for Arkansas, always being obedient to His leading. We stayed with our family, as our home was rented, and sought for direction.

We visited many churches, looking for somewhere truly spirit led, but could not find any direction from the Lord. Stuart was asking for a church that was all set up with leadership and everything in place, but he heard the Spirit say, "I haven't called you to a life of ease." That prophetic word, all those years ago, came back. "You're a pioneering couple, with a pioneering spirit." "So here we go again, Lord!" we said.

Stuart heard from the Lord to plant a church, but I was very reluctant, after the struggles we had encountered pioneering previously. However, the Lord reassured me that this would be different. So in May 2008, we planted an independent church, called "Spirit Life". Even the Lord had been involved in naming it. He said, "Call it *Spirit Life.*" Our son Ray, his family, and another couple came with us, and we planted it in Robina on the Gold Coast of Australia. We always had a heart for people and for extending God's kingdom.

Planting a church from scratch was not a small thing, but the Lord had spoken, so in faith we stepped out. Stuart began working for a pool building company and was leaving home at 4:00 am to travel for an hour to Brisbane. He would work a long day building swimming pools in the hot sun. Not an easy task at the age of 62.

Once, on a prayer night, only one business man attended and we proceeded to pray. The man spoke to us and asked Stuart if he could cease his manual work and just pastor the church.

Stuart was reducing his work to just three days per week in order for us to have sufficient funds to live from. A miracle happened this very night. The man said, "I will support you and pay you what you were earning over those three days and you can devote your time to pastoring." What a wonderful gesture! That truly was from the Lord.

With strong support, right from the start, Spirit Life was a joy, and indeed was different. God's provision was always there, and we had such a marvelous congregation, with all aspects of church life. Children's church and youth were strong, and God was blessing us. Spirit Life embraced our love for Arkansas and supported our vision with strong prayer.

After fourteen years of pastoring, there came a change of seasons again for us. We attended some special meetings at a local church. There was a specific prophecy that God had prepared the man who was going to pastor our church, and we received words of fresh direction for us again!

If it is truly the Lord, then as people of faith, we wanted to yield to His will. Any change is difficult to embrace and we were no different than most. Our love for the people and our relationships were hard to release, but release them we must. The whole process took a year, and Pastor Ken and Frances Wigglesworth established themselves on the Gold Coast. It is wonderful seeing the original vision still being upheld, and the love for the Holy Spirit in evidence in the meetings.

In April 2023, we planned our 17th return trip to Arkansas. We had been unable to return with covid restrictions, and so after a five-year break, we were preparing to go again. Twenty-three years older than our very first visit, we wanted to plan our trip well and not overload our itinerary.

We set off with a planned schedule of 25 meetings, knowing that this would probably be added to. It finished up expanding to 33 meetings, which was the maximum, and only one meeting out of the boundaries of Arkansas, to Greenville Mississippi.

It was prophesied by several, that this visit would be on a new level, and so with a high level of expectancy, we were excited to go again!

A quotation from the Bible:

Matthew 4:23
"And Jesus went about all of Galilee, teaching in

their synagogues, preaching the gospel of the king-
dom and healing all kinds of sickness and all kinds
of disease among the people."

John 21:25
"And there are also many other things that Jesus
did, which if they were written one by one, I sup-
pose that even the world itself could not contain
the books that would be written. Amen."

Jesus wants us to be obedient. I hate to think what would
have happened if we had not done all the Lord asked of us.
The stories of our experiences and touching so many lives,
some of which we have never been told, and the joy of hearing testimonies, spurs us on in our walk of obedience for the
Lord.

Chapter 22
Testimonies

On our visit in 2023, we were privileged to hear the personal account of a young man's healing that happened in 2018. Caleb Stockton was rushed to the hospital in Fort Smith on a Friday, with bi-lateral, severe pneumonia. All of his five lobes were completely white, and he was having congestive heart failure. His oxygen levels were in the 40's, and doctors were talking about a by-pass. Two day later, on a Sunday, he was put into an induced coma and his body was shutting down. Doctors were telling his parents that there was nothing more they could do for Caleb.

In church, at Cedarville, on that Sunday morning, Stuart had a word of knowledge that someone had a very serious upper respiratory infection and he was calling for this person to come. "Come and get your healing.", Stuart called.

Of course, Caleb was in the hospital and could hardly do that, but he had a good buddy who responded and went to stand in for him. The church prayed for Caleb's healing. God began to work a miracle and by the end of the week, Caleb was released from hospital. He told us that further x-ray's, showed all five lobes were completely clean. Doctors said they looked like a baby's lungs, showing absolutely no scar tissue at all, which would not have been the case had it not been for God's touch.

We would never have learned the facts of Caleb's healing had we not returned to this church. This has happened all over Arkansas. When we return, we hear these wonderful stories! We have prayed for so many people in this state, and have believed for their healing.

Many healings have taken place in Charleston Life Church. Brother Harold, the pastor's father, had very painful hands. The skin on his hands were cracked and always splitting. They would bleed at night, and Brother Harold had to wear gloves to bed, so he wouldn't scratch them, and make them bleed. This had gone on for fifteen years. Brother Harold had been to doctors, and had tried many ointments and creams to heal them.

Nothing seemed to work. He even had ointment at church so he could apply to his hands. It was impossible to clap his hands. It also made working very difficult. On one visit to the Church, Stuart and I prayed for Brother Harold, applied some anointing oil, and had him rub his hands together. On our return visit, here was a very happy man, holding out his hands to show us they were totally healed. Jesus was the Healer! That was twelve years ago.

Another brother, Dennis, broke his back 21 years ago, and was reluctant to have back surgery. We prayed and Dennis felt something physically happen in his spine from his L1 to L6. He said it felt like a zipper was zipping up. He's not sure if it was an expansion, or a contraction. In his job as a ware-house manager, his back gets a lot of hard work. All the pain left, and he was healed! Praise God!

An extremely thin lady came for prayer, and I thought she was close to death's door. Her son stayed right beside her and really seemed anxious for his mother. We prayed for her, and she lay on the floor for quite some time. My heart went out to her, in her extremely weakened state, as she lay in her track suit.

The very next night, I couldn't believe the transformation. "Was this indeed the same person? How could this be?", I thought. This beautifully dressed lady, nicely made up in a lovely colorful suit, stockings and high heeled shoes, came to the altar again to receive more healing. I could scarcely believe the transformation before my eyes! She was beaming with joy.

So many in the meetings in this church have been healed. I've lost count over the years of our visits. A dear lady, Kim, was battling Hepatitis C. The irritation to her skin was so severe and she would even attempt to scratch her back until it bled. Her bed sheets would be covered with blood. Kim was totally healed. Another time, Kim was battling cancer. The Lord was her Healer, and after we prayed and stood in faith with her, Kim told us she was cancer free! God was so good.

Brother Kenny, was battling multiple sclerosis and walking with a cane. His doctor wanted him to use a walker, but Kenny refused. People had told Kenny to come to Life Church for healing, and Kenny, although skeptical, came. He told us he was thinking, "What have I got to lose?" He had everything to gain!

I remember praying for him with Stuart on the first night. God was touching him mightily. The second night he was there again. He lay under the anointing, God touching him again. One could see the change in his body, and he seemed to be getting stronger physically. What we didn't know until recently, was that Kenny had battled addictions and alcohol for 40 years. These had taken a great toll on his body, and now God was setting him free! What a miracle working God! No medications, no limp, and a living testimony to the goodness of God.

A young lady, by the name of Jaime, came for prayer when we ministered at The Ridge. She had pain in her left shoulder, back, and neck. Jaime experienced fire coming down her body and she has been walking in recovery ever since. Jaime shared that when she feels tingles of pain trying to settle on her body, she strongly resists, and claims her healing in Jesus' Name.

She continues to have complete arm movement in her left arm, whereas before the prayer, there was none. I was so impressed with Jaime's testimony. She used her Facebook media to her full advantage, giving regular updates, and sharing her healing to all her contacts. What a marvelous testimony it was, and so powerful!

We were recently in Pine Bluff Assembly for the very first time, when Stuart called for people dealing with leukemia. I had never heard him call for that before. Two people immediately ran to the altar. One lady for her niece, who was in hospital in Dallas Texas. She had been near death twice. We prayed in faith. It was wonderful to hear the results! She had received a text. "My niece is doing well, and she is eating.", she told us.

Her kidneys had stopped working, and are now functioning. In addition, her blood pressure is now normal and she needs no more medication for blood pressure. Thank you, Jesus!

The other lady that responded stood in for her brother. Later, he reported, for the very first time in months, he had an appetite. He held down his breakfast and was feeling that all the signs of leukemia had left his body. We certainly stand with these folk and believe for a total healing.

We were invited to do a television show at Bro Akers' church which would be aired in the West Monroe TV station. When we arrived, he was in tremendous pain and could only stand by holding onto his desk. He was so ill. It was obvious by the color of his skin. He had Crohn's disease.

We laid hands on him and prayed, then we did the recording. Afterward, Brother Akers began to run around the church! He ran and ran and we cheered him on, with Stuart joining in with him. God had healed him. Hallelujah! This was a different man to the one we had met earlier. We went out to eat together and to have fellowship. He ate a hearty meal, totally healed!

Our friend, Duane, came for prayer for a tooth that had a cavity. We had prayed for many with problem teeth and had seen miracles. The very next day, Duane went to his dentist and there was no cavity!

We have, on occasion, seen gold dust appearing on clothes and shoes. Stuart, Duane and his son, Rodney have experienced this.

God was using our meetings to connect people. One young couple had met each other when they attended our services. They are in full-time ministry today and God is using them powerfully! This has happened several times, to our knowledge.

I have a personal testimony where the Lord has taken care of our personal needs. I remember going to the dentist in Australia for problems with my teeth. While working on my teeth, he told me he had some bad news. It was going to cost two-thousand dollars to fix two teeth!

I felt apprehensive going home to tell Stuart, because I knew his teeth were in worse condition than mine. Stuart's reply was, "We will just have to believe God to supply." And so we committed it to prayer.

We were on one of our earlier visits to Arkansas and we were in a church in the North West area of the state. When the children find out where we are from they love to ask questions about Steve Irwin, kangaroos, koalas, and crocodiles. A dad came to chat with me and he asked how my week had been. I told him I had been to see a dentist because of a toothache. He replied, "I am a dentist and I will take care of your teeth."

The Lord has truly blessed us through this man and His love for the Lord. We have had a lot of dental work done and have had many crowns and bridge work done for Stuart where teeth had been previously pulled.

"Thank you Dr. Paul. You were truly an answer to prayer and are a dear friend who has welcomed us into your home along with your family. The Lord hears your cry and answers your prayers."

> *Luke 7:21-22*
> *"And that very hour He cured many people of their infirmities, afflictions, and evil spirits, and to many who were blind, He gave sight. Then Jesus answered and said to them, 'Go and tell John the things you've seen and heard: that the blind see, the lame walk, the lepers are cleansed, the deaf hear, the dead are raised, the poor have the gospel preached to them.'"*

So, you can see from these scriptures, that God is a miracle working God. A God of the Supernatural, and all things are possible to them who believe! As you read this, would you believe for your miracle right now?

Pray, believe and receive! Stuart always says, "One of the greatest ways to get healed is to pray for yourself, releasing your faith, and reaching out to this Jesus, who can heal you."

Chapter 23
Having Done All to Stand

The battle was great in the invisible realm. Opposition was strong and the cost to walk in obedience has been enormous. I'm not referring to monetary cost. The devil was not happy, and we knew as much.

> *Ephesians 6:12-13*
> *"For we do not wrestle against flesh and blood, but against principalities and powers, against the rulers of the darkness of this age against the spiritual hosts of wickedness in the heavenly places.*
>
> *Therefore, take up the whole armor of God, that you may be able to withstand in the evil day, and having done all to stand."*

What God is looking for is a willing heart, a humble spirit and a committed life. These things may actually go a lot further than a list of educational credentials.

Jesus disciples left all and followed Him (Luke 5:10-11).

We all make choices in our lives. A plaque we had on our wall in New Zealand read:

> *"Choose this day whom you will serve, but as for me and my house, we will serve the Lord." Joshua 24:15*

Our walk has been by faith, and your walk is by faith. Consistency is important. Over fifty years we have been steadfast in our faith. God is developing us all and we never stop learning as we go. Arkansas was His idea, and we were willing and obedient.

He was working a wonderful healing in my life, for which I am ever so grateful. Night after night, as we went from church-to-church ministering, Stuart would have me come to the platform and share what I felt the Holy Spirit would have me share. I depended on Him heavily to be my strength, and give me the words, speaking boldly without stammering and standing against fear that would try to grip my life. No one knew the battle I was having.

I remembered the pastor that stayed in our home so many years ago (in the 1970's) saying, "When you begin to preach, God will heal you."

Between the front row and the pulpit, I never knew what I was going to say, but each time became easier and easier and my confidence grew! God was indeed bringing healing to my speech and a renewed boldness to my life.

Stuart saw the healing taking place, right before his eyes. Of course, a lot of other things contributed to this over the years. I never thought it would take a lifetime to eventuate.

Don't ever give up on receiving your healing, thinking that the Lord has forgotten you. He wants us to be whole, and healed in every way! By His Stripes I am healed, and by His

Stripes I was healed when Jesus went to the cross 2000 years ago. All I had to do was appropriate His healing, the finished work of the Cross.

> JUST THINK: (A verse I have treasured for years)
> *"Just think, you're not here by chance, But by God's choosing. His hand formed you and made you the person you are. He compares you to no one else. You are one of a kind..."* — Roy Lessin

You lack nothing that His grace can't give you. He has allowed you to be here at this time in history to fulfill His special purpose for this generation. Of all the miracles we have seen and all that the Lord has done, the greatest of all is the gift of Salvation, when a person acknowledges and receives Jesus Christ as their Lord and Savior.

The Bible tells us our names are written in the Lamb's Book of Life, and God takes our hearts of stone and gives us hearts of flesh. He writes His ways on the tablets of our hearts.

John 3:7 Jesus says, "You must be born again." This is the only reference in the Bible, where Jesus said, "You must."

Our journey began when we gave our hearts to Jesus and were born again of the Spirit of God. He changed our lives and put us on an incredible journey of fulfillment.

As you are reading this, our prayer for you would be that you would come into all that the Lord has for your life and that you would have the courage to pray this prayer, maybe for the very first time in your life.

Pray this prayer: "Lord Jesus, I receive you today as my Lord and Savior. I ask you to forgive me of all my sins and wash me clean in your Blood. I thank you, that you died for me."

Romans 10:9
"If you confess with your mouth, the Lord Jesus and believe in your heart that God has raised Him from the dead, you will be saved."

Verse 10
"For with the heart one believes unto righteous-ness, and with the mouth confession is made unto salvation."

The next step is to find a good Spirit-filled church where you can meet other Christians and grow spiritually.

One word from the Lord, "Arkansas", and He changed our lives. We will never stop praying and seeking for Revival to sweep the State of Arkansas.

We thank the Lord for all those that have been a part of our journey and have touched our lives in an incredible way. People have stood with us in prayer and helped us to carry the message of Good News.

Arkansas
Forever in our Heart

We would love to hear your testimonies!

Contact us at:

Colleen Price
eagleprice@hotmail.com

Stuart Price
Pricestuart2@gmail.com

Made in the USA
Columbia, SC
19 August 2024

40229167R00065